W9-BGL-373

Reach
for the
Top

The Harvard Business Review Book Series

Designing and Managing Your Career, Edited by Harry Levinson

Ethics in Practice: Managing the Moral Corporation, Edited by Kenneth R. Andrews

Managing Projects and Programs, With a Preface by Norman R. Augustine

Manage People, Not Personnel: Motivation and Performance Appraisal, With a Preface by Victor H. Vroom

Revolution in Real Time: Managing Information Technology in the 1990s, With a Preface by William G. McGowan

Strategy: Seeking and Securing Competitive Advantage, Edited with an Introduction by Cynthia A. Montgomery and Michael E. Porter

Leaders on Leadership: Interviews with Top Executives, With a Preface by Warren Bennis

Seeking Customers, Edited with an Introduction by Benson P. Shapiro and John J. Sviokla

Keeping Customers, Edited with an Introduction by John J. Sviokla and Benson P. Shapiro

The Learning Imperative: Managing People for Continuous Innovation, Edited with an Introduction by Robert Howard

The Articulate Executive: Orchestrating Effective Communication, With a Preface by Fernando Bartolomé

Differences That Work: Organization Excellence through Diversity, Edited with an Introduction by Mary C. Gentile

Reach for the Top: Women and the Changing Facts of Work Life, Edited with an Introduction by Nancy A. Nichols

Reach for the Top

Women and the Changing Facts of Work Life

Edited with
an Introduction by
Nancy A. Nichols

Foreword by
Rosabeth Moss Kanter

A Harvard Business Review Book

Copyright © 1977, 1982, 1987, 1989, 1990, 1991, 1992, 1993, 1994 by the President and Fellows of Harvard College.
All rights reserved
Printed in the United States of America

98 97 96 95 94   5 4 3 2 1

All rights reserved. No part of this book may be reproduced, stored in a retrieval system, or transmitted, in any form or by any means, electronic, mechanical, photocopying, recording, or otherwise without the prior written permission of the copyright holder.

The *Harvard Business Review* articles in this collection are available as individual reprints. Discounts apply to quantity purchases. For information and ordering contact Operations Department, Harvard Business School Publishing Corporation, Boston, MA 02163. Telephone: (617) 495-6192, 9 a.m. to 5 p.m. Eastern Time, Monday through Friday. Fax: (617) 495-6985, 24 hours a day.

The paper used in this publication meets the requirements of the American National Standard for Permanence of Paper for Printed Library Materials Z39.48-1984

Library of Congress Cataloging-in-Publication Data

Reach for the top : women and the changing facts of work life/edited, with an introduction by Nancy A. Nichols : foreword by Rosabeth Moss Kanter.
    p.   cm. — (A Harvard business review book)
  Includes bibliographical references and index.
  ISBN 0-87584-507-X (alk. paper)
    1. Women executives—United States. 2. Sex role in the work environment—United States. 3. Sex discrimination in employment—United States. 4. Women—Employment—United States.   I. Nichols, Nancy A., 1959–   . II. Series: Harvard business review book series.
  HD6054.4.U6R43 1994
    331.4′0973—dc20   93-34718
                                                                          CIP

Contents

Foreword   ix
Rosabeth Moss Kanter

Introduction   xiii
Nancy A. Nichols

Part I Breaking the Double Bind

1 Whatever Happened to Rosie the Riveter?   3
Nancy A. Nichols
During Word War II, an unprecedented number of
women followed Rosie onto the factory floor, only to
be forced to leave when the GIs returned from the
war. Decades later, managerial women continue to
battle against the same kinds of discrimination and
gender bias.

2 Ways Women Lead   13
Judith B. Rosener
Women managers who have broken the glass ceiling
in midsized nontraditional organizations are—
succeeding because of—not in spite of—certain
characteristics generally considered to be "feminine."
In a highly controversial article, Rosener details the
"special" skills of women managers.

3 Two Women, Three Men on a Raft   **25**
Robert Schrank
One week on a raft going down the Rogue River sets
the stage for a study in gender styles and leadership
issues. Women trying to navigate in a changing
organizational structure will find this trip down the
river enlightening.

Part II   Fitting In or Fighting Back

1 The Case of the Mismanaged Ms.   **41**
Sally Seymour
Ruth Linsky gets passed over for a job as marketing
director. Under pressure, her boss reveals a whole
host of sexually biased reasons for promoting a man
into the position, including the familiar: "She'll just
get married and leave and have a baby."

2 The Case of the Hidden Harassment   **63**
Daniel Niven
Manager Jerry Tarkwell accidentally learns that Jill
McNair is being sexually harassed. When he tries to
help, he's told to mind his own business. This case
raises issues of accountability and responsibility for
managers and pits them against the privacy needs of
employees.

3 The Memo Every Woman Keeps in Her Desk   **75**
Kathleen Reardon
With the resignation of two senior women, Liz Ames
decides to address the climate of female failure in her
corporation with a memo to the boss. In it, she says,
"I can't help but detect a disturbing pattern. Why do
such capable, conscientious women who have
demonstrated intense commitment to their careers
suddenly want to change course or spend more time
at home?"

Part III   The Balancing Act

**1 Management Women and
the New Facts of Life**   **87**
Felice N. Schwartz
"The cost of employing women in management is
greater than the cost of employing men." This simple
statement set off a national debate as Schwartz went
on to argue for a "Mommy Track" that would
separate would-be mothers from fast-track career
women.

2 Mother's Work   **103**
Nan Stone
An incisive essay that draws on recent texts to answer
the question: What happens at home—to the family,
to children—when both father and mother work
full-time?

3 The Case of the Part-Time Partner   **113**
Gary W. Loveman
When Julie Ross, a part-time associate at Meeker,
Needham & Ames, applies for partnership, a
full-fledged debate breaks out over what kind of
commitment is necessary to "make it" at the firm. As
this case demonstrates, women who attempt to
balance home and workplace pressures by working
part-time sometimes get left behind.

Part IV   Tales from the Front

1 From the Classroom to the Corner Office   **131**
Rosemarie B. Greco
A sex-discrimination suit helped Greco see the unfair
practices at her bank. But it wasn't until she became
head of human resources, and eventually CEO, that
she could actually begin to change them.

2 The Purpose at the Heart of Management   **143**
Kye Anderson
Kye Anderson knew no glass ceiling. Compelled by
the death of her father, she created a medical
technology company able to save lives, but not
without it taking some toll on her own. "I'd leave my
two young children at home and fly off to a meeting
in California and cry all the way to the coast,
thinking, 'I should be home taking care of my kids.'"

**3 The Entrepreneur Sees Herself as Manager:
An Interview with Lore Harp**   **157**
Eliza G. C. Collins
Lore Harp did it the hard way. She started Vector
Graphics on her kitchen table and turned her $6,000
investment into a $25 million company. But, she says,
"I'm not a feminist . . . I feel that most women gain
acceptance from peers, male or female, by proving
integrity and intelligence—not by talking about job
discrimination and all sorts of other complaints. I just
don't have time for that."

About the Contributors   **177**

Index   **181**

Foreword

Rosabeth Moss Kanter

In the single largest demographic phenomenon of the past half-century, women have taken their place side-by-side with men in the workplace, changing the look if not the spirit of business. Their increasing power as they reach for the top—to use Nancy Nichols' excellent image—has prompted the *Harvard Business Review* to examine this phenomenon. *HBR*'s mission is to convey cutting-edge ideas before they become conventional wisdom, to provoke debate that helps thoughtful managers challenge their assumptions.

It is in that spirit that Nichols has collected *HBR*'s best analyses, most current advice, successful role models, and controversial issues. Together they raise a provocative set of questions. Do women manage differently from men? Can demanding careers accommodate family needs? How should companies encourage potential leaders who do not fit a single mold? Questions like these are often raised first in the United States, but their relevance should be clear to managers and companies throughout the world, as competitive pressures put human resource issues on center stage nearly everywhere.

Today both women and men have a stake in equal opportunity issues. Full development of human resources is a key competitive advantage in the knowledge society. Meritocracy—letting talent rise to the top regardless of where it is found and whether it is male or female—is essential to business success in free-market economies. Within this context, the equality of women in the work force is no longer a politically correct luxury. It has become a competitive necessity.

Yet even as equal opportunity becomes a more urgent priority, the shifting economy is creating new challenges for women and the companies who employ them. Indeed, the changing economy has created a new prism through which to examine the important issues raised in this volume.

Today, women must rely on themselves rather than on institutions to create careers. They must be entrepreneurs who make their own opportunities—either within or outside of a major corporation—or professionals with portable career assets—skills and reputations that can be applied anywhere.

This is in sharp contrast to the situation ten years ago when progress seemed assured if only corporations would create career ladders for women. The common wisdom at that time was that if women entered large, established corporations, their economic security, if not a top position, was ensured. But now the decline and downsizing of many corporate giants has changed the situation, dramatically heightening the pressure on women reaching for the top.

Jobs in large companies are being shed not one by one but by the thousands and ten thousands. In these organizations, issues of power and acceptance will become even more important for women. Men, accustomed to security, are unlikely to welcome more competitors for fewer, less-secure positions, making it even more difficult for women, who already report receiving a cold reception in corporate America.

For example, at one company a colleague studied, senior women professionals reported that "casual sexism" was pervasive. Each woman cited examples of insulting or biased behavior that was culturally acceptable and largely unnoticed, from jokes to thoughtless remarks. Most of the women just ignored them. In this regard, Kathleen Reardon's case, "The Memo Every Woman Keeps in Her Desk" in Part II, is more than relevant, it is a sort of survival guide for women in the 1990s.

While the message of this book—that women are caught in the midst of unprecedented social and economic changes—will not come as a surprise to women who cope with these upheavals daily, the advice and solutions within can help women grapple with vast changes in their organizations.

For entrepreneurs, professionals, and, increasingly, for corporate managers, power today derives less from the job itself and more from networks and connections—the ability to wield influence outside of the formal work arena.

For executive men, the path to power is still straightforward: join the usual clubs, boards of directors, civic associations, visible charities, or national leadership groups. Then leverage ties with financiers, power brokers, ranking politicians, competitor CEOs, opinion leaders, or possible venture partners to bring benefits to the company.

For executive women, however, membership in these higher circles is just beginning. Harvard Professor Herminia Ibarra found that, despite the significant achievements of women, men were still better able to convert professional contacts outside the company into centrality inside the company.

The result: women, trapped between powerful social and economic forces, are leaving the corporate world in droves. Indeed, the traditional indifference with which women have been greeted in corporations and the emergence of small business as an economic powerhouse have created a new and inspired group of female entrepreneurs, two of whom—Kye Anderson and Lore Harp—we hear from in this collection.

Women-owned businesses have grown both in numbers and revenue throughout the 1980s and early 1990s. According to the Small Business Administration, women owned 32% of the sole proprietorships in 1990, up from 26% in 1980, and were expected to form businesses 1.5 times faster than men in the 1990s. Being in business for themselves makes it possible for women to call the shots, set their own flexible schedules to accommodate parenting or other personal needs, and contribute to the economy through the creation of new jobs.

Indeed some authors in the volume will argue that women bring special managerial skills to the new workplace. Yet these theories are both controversial and dangerous. Stereotyping women as different-superior is just as limiting as stereotyping them as different-inferior.

I continue to believe that women and men operating under similar expectations and in similar situations behave in similar ways. The "heroines" of Nancy Nichols' book—Rosemarie Greco, Kye Anderson, and Lore Harp—certainly prove that women have numerous leadership strengths. But even more: they show how women, given opportunities to use their talents, can create remarkable innovations that make extraordinary contributions to their companies, customers, and the world around them.

For that reason and many more, *Reach for the Top* is an inspiring collection that can help launch the next half-century of women's accomplishments in this swiftly changing world.

Introduction

Nancy A. Nichols

Since the late 1970s when women began to join the work force in earnest, the *Harvard Business Review* has examined their impact on the corporation. For the past 20 years, *HBR* has merged its essential understanding of the managerial world with its deep respect for the abilities of women managers. The 12 articles in this volume represent the best of that effort. By drawing on the work of both male and female authors from varying viewpoints and experiences, *Reach for the Top* offers readers a unique view of the complex mix of opportunities and limitations—both real and perceived—that exists for women in organizations today.

And while this volume offers no easy answers to problems such as sexual harassment or sexual discrimination, it does present a wide range of solutions from which each woman must choose. For the very first thing that a woman must learn to manage is her femininity. From the moment she enters the work force until the day she leaves the corporate arena, she is judged not just as a manager *on* the job, but as a woman *in* the job.

Women today face enormous pressures to squeeze themselves into organizations that are most often controlled by men and into managerial roles that have come to be defined in almost entirely masculine terms. In order to be successful, women must carefully thread their way through a contradictory set of complex expectations, constantly balancing their own and others' beliefs about what it means to be a woman with long-held beliefs about what it means to be a manager, a lawyer, or just about any other type of professional.

As Felice Schwartz, former president of the women's not-for-profit research organization Catalyst, writes, "Women can never feel secure about how they should dress and act, whether they should speak out or grin and bear it when they encounter discrimination, stereotyping, sexual harassment, and paternalism. Social interaction and travel with male colleagues and with male clients can be charged. As they move up, the normal increase in pressure and responsibility is compounded for women because they are women."

In fact, as Schwartz suggests, there is almost no acceptable way for a woman to bridge the gap between her feminine nature and the traditional "masculine" demands of the managerial role. If, for example, a woman attempts to fit herself into that role by acting like a man, she is forced to act in a sexually dissonant way. However, a woman who acts in a "feminine" manner, speaking quietly and deferring to her male colleagues, risks being seen as ineffective, or worse, getting trampled on the way to the top.

Breaking the Double Bind

It is this double bind that defines the problem women face at work every day. In Part I of *Reach for the Top* we take a searching look at the historical relationship between gender and the managerial role—a link that was established about the turn of the century and went largely unchallenged until the beginning of World War II.

During the war, women were forced to take on many of the roles that men had traditionally played. As a result, they became key players as American industry switched from peace-time to war-time production. For example, there were never more than 45 women workers out of a monthly average of 80,000 employees at Ford's massive River Rouge plant before the war. Yet by the middle of the war, women accounted for 12% of the work force at River Rouge, where they performed a variety of tasks, including riveting. Rosie the Riveter thus became a war-time hero and her rallying cry, "We can do it," spurred factory women to exceed all previous productivity records.

However, when the war was over and Ford, and the rest of the country, made the switch to peace-time production, women were laid off in large numbers. Even though they had shown themselves capable workers, often more efficient than the men who had preceded them, the prejudice persisted that factory work was men's work. The brief amount of time that women spent riveting was not enough to change our cultural perception of factory work from "men's" work to women's "work."

As I argue in my essay,"Whatever Happened to Rosie the Riveter?," women managers face much the same problem today. Managerial work continues to be defined by what our society deems masculine tendencies: assertiveness and a tough-minded and analytical stance toward problems. Women trying to fit themselves into the managerial role must therefore find a way to fit into this masculine mold.

It is no easy task as the women on a rafting expedition with Robert Schrank can attest to. In "Two Women, Three Men on a Raft," Schrank and his male partner on a trip down the Rogue River are so uncomfortable with the idea of a woman at the helm that they actively try to undermine their female rafting partners. A series of nods and grimaces between the men serves as a secret signal for them to take over.

"Once we had established that things were not going well," writes Schrank, "we then felt free to take our own corrective measures, such as trying to steer the raft from our forward paddle positions, an almost impossible thing to do. Not only is running the raft from the front not at all helpful to the person at the helm, but also if the helmsperson is not aware of the counterforces, the raft can easily turn around like a carousel. The unaware helmsperson is then totally out of control."

Ultimately, the men's reluctance to let the women lead becomes a self-fulfilling prophecy and the women suddenly are *unable* to lead. The raft capsizes as much from the turmoil on board as from the rushing water that surrounds them.

Yet women who sense the resistance that the women on the raft experienced and purposefully do not exhibit a male authoritarian style may fare no better. In a controversial article ("Ways Women Lead") that has been both criticized openly and broadly acclaimed, Judith Rosener delineates a second wave of women managers who exhibit what she refers to as an "interactive leadership" style. According to Rosener, "These women actively work to make their interactions with subordinates positive for everyone involved. More specifically, the women encourage participation, share power and information, enhance other people's self-worth, and get others excited about their work." It is these kinds of nurturing behaviors—and Rosener's ground-breaking work—that have come to define the new "feminine style" of leadership.

While the feminine style of leadership is both a more successful and comfortable style for some women, it is eerily reminiscent of the not-so-distant past when women were allowed only those nurturing roles. "These are negative stereotypes with positive labels," one critic told the *New York Times*.

By freeing women from the need to manage like men, we may have landed them in another more difficult prison. Forcing them to manage like women by taking on the additional role of nurturing and caring for their employees may condemn them only to the roles reserved for people dealing with emotions in the corporation.

In addition, demanding that women manage like women hampers those who would like to manage like men. In my essay, I discuss the case of Ann Hopkins, a consultant at Price Waterhouse who was denied partnership because she failed to wear make-up, act feminine, and manage like a woman. At least one member of the senior managerial team told her that in order to make partner she would have to take charge less often—most unusual advice for an up-and-coming executive.

Indeed, by legitimizing and encouraging a female style of leadership, we have upped the stakes for women like Hopkins who must confront a set of contradictory expectations every day. An almost constant struggle to fit themselves into divergent roles weighs on women and weighs down the organizations they work for. Ann Hopkins chose to fight the discrimination that existed at her firm head on by filing suit. After a long legal battle, she succeeded in winning a partnership at the firm.

Yet the decision to confront hostile behavior openly may not be the best decision for all women in all situations. Hopkins, after all, suffered through nearly a decade of litigation after she filed suit.

Fitting In or Fighting Back

Far from being an academic issue, the decision to fight back—as Ann Hopkins did—or to fit in—as the women on the raft did—is a decision that women and their managers must deal with daily. And while it would be easy to come up with politically correct platitudes, the three cases in Part II of *Reach for the Top* reveal that there are no swift solutions when complex social and organizational issues clash and livelihoods and careers hang in the balance. In each case, a different set of circumstances and personalities emerges to paint a multidimensional picture of life in an organization.

In Sally Seymour's "The Case of the Mismanaged Ms." Ruth Linsky, sales director at Triton Industries, has just been passed over for a job as marketing director. When Linsky suspects that the reason she has been passed over has something to do with her gender, she storms into the office of the director of human resources, threatening to file "a sexual discrimination suit, a sexual harassment suit, and whatever other kind of suit she can come up with." The human resources director, also a woman, goes straight to the CEO, and together they confront Linsky's boss. He reveals a host of sexually biased reasons for promoting a man into the position, including the all-too-familiar: "Ruth will just get married and leave and have a baby." And the more blatant: "I don't think women work out as well as men in certain positions."

In what seems like a fairy-tale ending to this case, the CEO finally "gets it" and from his sympathetic response, it is clear that something will be done. But it is necessary to add a cautionary note: even in situations where male executives are open to and actively seeking to create a just and equitable environment for women, changing the corporate culture can be a momentous task.

That is the message in Dan Niven's "The Case of the Hidden Harassment." When manager Jerry Tarkwell accidentally learns that Jill McNair is being sexually harassed, he tries to help, but she tells him to mind his own business. What follows is a heated debate that pits a manager's responsibility to the larger goals and culture of the company against an employee's right to solve her own problems.

Commentator Cheryl Wang, herself a victim of sexual harassment, advises Tarkwell, "You won't be helping Jill by forcing her to bring a complaint against the harasser. She is already a victim of someone else's unwanted actions. Don't compound her sense of victimization by pushing her into another situation she doesn't want to be in."

However, another commentator, Mikiko Taga, who has been instrumental in making the Japanese aware of the prevalence of sexual harassment, strongly disagrees. She tells McNair, "Doing nothing is not an option."

As these commentaries illustrate, even when there is blatant harassment that even the most senior managers of the company find intolerable, changing the corporate culture or even trying to mitigate the situation can be difficult. But what about situations where senior management is either ignorant or complacent? Is there hope for change? Or should women simply give up and go home as so many women are choosing to do in the 1990s.

In perhaps the most compelling case in this volume, "The Memo Every Woman Keeps in Her Desk," Kathleen Reardon describes a situation where a subtle form of sabotage is causing high-level, high-powered women to leave Vision Software. After two senior women resign, marketing executive Liz Ames writes a fiery memo to the CEO. "At meetings," writes Liz, "women are often talked over and interrupted; their ideas never seem to be heard. Last week, I attended a meeting with ten men and one other woman. As soon as the woman started her presentation, several side conversations began. Her presentation skills were excellent, but she couldn't seem to get people's attention."

What Reardon is describing at Vision Software is a culture that fails to acknowledge women or their contributions. Not unlike the situation on the raft, there is a consistent tide of resentment that is dragging women down and ultimately forcing them out. Yet these behaviors are so strongly ingrained in the culture of the company that fighting them may prove a hopeless battle.

Reardon's memo is tough, all right, but should she send it? Dozens of *HBR* readers weighed in. Many of the women had encountered similar situations, and, of those who had protested, more than a few had been fired for it. Our own commentators were divided about what Liz should do. Several, including author and feminist activist Gloria Steinem, thought she should send the memo. Steinem says, "Unless Liz is in imminent danger of hunger or homelessness, I would advise her to send the memo. If she doesn't, she is not only acting against her own and other women's long-term interest but also failing to give her company her best advice."

Jay Jackman, a psychiatrist and organizational consultant, vehemently disagreed. He thought Liz should seek support before sending the memo. "The undermining of women in the workplace is both common and difficult to change," writes Jackman. "It stems from a complicated interaction of men's beliefs and behaviors, women's beliefs and behaviors, the structures and procedures set up by companies, and the ways in which we organize and run our families."

Faced with the kind of entrenched corporate culture that Jackman is describing, many women simply opt out of the hierarchy, starting ventures of their own or searching for greener pastures. There is no question that both the women and the organizations suffer when that happens. Women are forced to abandon years of investment in a particular company, while the corporation loses a well-trained employee. But more important, the company loses an opportunity to learn about the environment in which their employees must operate when it refuses to hear negative feedback.

The Balancing Act

The stress that women feel at work is compounded when there are children at home. Indeed, while many women leave corporations because they are simply fed up with trying to fight back or exhausted from trying to fit in, many more leave to raise children. Perhaps the biggest brain drain facing corporations today is the stampede of young, well-trained women choosing baby bottles over boardrooms. The result, according to Felice Schwartz, is that women have become more expensive than men to hire.

Her landmark article, "Management Women and the New Facts of Life," leads off Part III. In it, she begins by admitting that women at work face a tougher road than men do. Yet, for Schwartz the solution lies not so much with changing the corporate culture—or building corporate day care centers—as it does with finding the right kind of woman to withstand the pressure. Her suggestion to companies is simple: decide early on which women can make the grade and then create two separate career tracks—one for women who are single-mindedly devoted to their work and another, which the *New York Times* quickly dubbed the Mommy Track, for those who plan to have children.

Yet Schwartz's plan had a fatal flaw. Few women can tell at 22 that they plan to have children at 34 and, even if they are prescient enough to have that kind of confidential chat with a human resources officer, it may be illegal to refuse them the same kinds of training, promotions, and opportunities to relocate that their male colleagues are given.

Although Schwartz's overly prescriptive plan proved unworkable, the need remains for companies to plan for pregnancy in a clear and foresightful way. A growing number of firms allow parents the opportunity to work part-time. Yet many women fear taking this option, even when it is available. Nan Stone, in her review of Arlie Hochschild's book, *The Second Shift*, describes a study of ten working couples conducted by a University of California professor over an eight-year period.

While two of the women whom Hochschild followed worked for a company that offered flextime, job sharing, and part-time work, neither felt free to partake of it. As Stone tells it, "Neither of these women felt free to work part-time—not because their jobs would not allow it but because their colleagues (male and female) would not countenance it. The message they got was clear: managers showed commitment by working long hours."

Indeed, women who opt to work part-time may find that their careers have become permanently derailed. In "The Case of the Part-Time Partner," by Gary Loveman, the law firm of Meeker, Needham & Ames, faces a crisis when part-time associate Julie Ross applies for a partnership. Because the issue of a partnership was not discussed when Julie went part-time, her candidacy has become a divisive issue for the firm and her career is in jeopardy.

Are women who work part-time as dedicated to the firm as women who work full-time, and should they be rewarded with a partnership? The management committee must decide, but even our expert commentators were divided. A woman partner in a New York law firm wrote: "Most women who have attained a level of professional success have done so by consciously sacrificing other aspects of their lives— whether it be marriage, children, or community involvement. . . . Creating a new set of partnership criteria for part-time associates, most of whom will be women, risks alienating women who have earned their status in the traditional way and have made the sacrifices Julie Ross was unwilling to make."

Still, if the firm fails to make Ross a partner, it risks losing the investment it has made in her skills and talents. As lawyer Barbara Mendel Mayden wrote, "Experience, expertise, and other effects of tenure that Ross gained while working an alternative schedule should not fall into a black hole."

As this case illustrates, the demands of motherhood often clash head on with the demands of a culture that assumes 12–15 hour days as a demonstration of loyalty and commitment. Viewed in this light, motherhood is just another barrier for women who must be able to fit themselves into jobs that were originally designed for men with wives at home.

Organizations have clearly failed to catch up with the vast social movements that have forever changed the American landscape. In her essay, Stone writes, "As in every social revolution, people's lives have changed more quickly than institutions—or individual psyches. . . . So for every working parent, the question remains: How do I balance home and work? Can I be a good manager or lawyer or editor and still be a good mom or dad?"

As Stone readily admits, the answer to those questions is both a personal and a corporate one. While parents must make their own choices about how they spend their time, employers can make a difference. Day care, part-time work, and flexible hours are only the beginning for Stone, who envisions some sweeping changes in the way we think about success. "It is time," she writes, "to rethink the logic that equates long hours with superior performance and workaholism with commitment."

Few women can evade the forces that are changing both their home and professional lives and in that sense the problem for women in the work world is one that must be addressed at the corporate level. Yet ironically the solution to the problem must always be an individual one. As Stone reminds us, "We live history even as we make it."

Tales from the Front

In Part IV we see how three successful women have coped with these social changes, making history as they broke the glass ceiling in banking, and pioneered in the male-dominated fields of medical technology and computer manufacturing. The three women profiled here both shaped and were shaped by the shifting social changes that brought women into the work force. Their stories, therefore, are not simply representative of their own struggles to reach the top. Rather, they represent the kinds of battles each woman must wage as she struggles toward success.

Rosemarie Greco lost a few battles as she made her way from secretary to CEO at a major bank in Philadelphia, but she won the war. In "From the Classroom to the Corner Office," Greco begins by happily training Vietnam War veterans to take managerial positions at twice her pay. Later her boss takes her memo containing her ideas for training at the bank and, using correction fluid, actually removes her name and places his own on it. He rationalizes his act by telling Greco, "Well, I knew you would want what was best for the bank, and your ideas would never have been implemented coming from so far down the ladder."

It isn't until another employee files suit, however, that Greco begins to see the practices at her bank as discriminatory. As part of the settlement agreement, the bank agrees to create a job-grading system for all professionals to ensure that women and minority members are fairly paid and have an opportunity for promotion. However, when she began to slot employees according to job descriptions, Greco begins to face facts. She writes: "Even in the same or similar jobs, the work of men was valued much more highly than that of women. Suddenly I realized that in teaching 'men only' to be branch managers when I was a secretary and in failing to translate my former boss's comment of 'from so far down the ladder' to 'because the ideas came from a woman,' I had been an unwitting accomplice in perpetuating Fidelity's corporate culture."

All that changed when Greco became head of human resources and later CEO of the bank. She fired the boss who stole her ideas and made her bank one of the best places in America for women to work.

While Greco was busy shattering the glass ceiling, Kye Anderson was pushing hard at the limitations of science. Watching her father die of a heart attack in the late 1950s, Anderson learned firsthand about the need for improved medical diagnostic equipment. To fulfill both a personal need and a clear demand in the marketplace, Anderson created Medical Graphics Corporation, a company on the cutting edge of cardiorespiratory diagnostics. Her company saved lives, but not without it taking some toll on her own. "I'd leave my two young children at home and fly off to a meeting in California and cry all the way to the coast thinking, I should be home taking care of my kids."

Lore Harp had the same guilty feelings when she started a company which assembled computer memory boards. After her road trip promoting the initial public offering of Vector Graphics, her children begged her to stay home more often.

In an interview entitled, "The Entrepreneur Sees Herself as Manager," Harp tells of success beyond her wildest dreams. Working at her kitchen table, she turned her $6,000 investment into a $25 million company. Yet her success not only took Harp away from her children, it also ended her marriage and several friendships. Within the industry she became known as "that bitch who is running the company."

Still says Harp, "I'm not a feminist. I feel that most women gain acceptance from peers, male or female, by proving integrity and intelligence—not by talking about job discrimination." Performance, after all, is a prerequisite to success.

Yet as these three stories illustrate, it is possible for women to succeed in many different ways: by battling their way up the corporate ladder, by becoming an entrepreneur, by fighting discrimination openly and fervently, and by turning a deaf ear to it, which is why dealing with the topic on a theoretical level is so difficult. There is no *one* right way and no *one* right answer. And yet there seems to exist one universal approach: women of all ages and in all fields must continue to reach for the top in an unrelenting desire to fulfill themselves, to serve their employers and their families, and to create economic prosperity for themselves, their companies, and their countries. That, after all, is the only true measure of success.

PART

I

Breaking the Double Bind

1
Whatever Happened to Rosie the Riveter?

Nancy A. Nichols

Rosie the Riveter is both a romantic and a heroic figure from the World War II era. A former housewife turned war hero, Rosie emerged from the kitchen and built the machinery necessary to fight and win World War II. Posters emblazoned with her picture became a symbol of wartime courage and patriotism. Her motto "We can do it!" stirred countless women.

And not only did Rosie do it, she did it better than anyone had ever done it before. Rosie was a key player in the retooling of U.S. industry from peacetime to wartime production. During the five years she was on the shop floor, from 1942 to 1947, productivity rose, product cycle time dropped, and quality improved.

Yet despite her success, Rosie was forced off the factory floor when the war ended, her achievements buried in books, all her accomplishments wiped out of our consciousness. She had proven her abilities, but she remained that cultural enigma: a woman in a man's job. Rosie's skills, which had helped win World War II, were deemed unnecessary in the fight for competitiveness that began about the time she left the factory. Rosie, it seemed, would have to spend the rest of her time baking cookies, not building machinery.

While Rosie may seem like a quaint historical figure to some people, her story contains prudent, even urgent, lessons for women in management today. For they too work in what have historically been "men's" jobs. As such, Rosie's story can help us understand the plight of modern managerial women. That's why we ask, whatever happened to Rosie the Riveter? And, more important, what can we learn from her?

Rosie Was Robbed!

During World War II, women were free to be men; they were even encouraged to be men. In the face of the fervent demands of wartime production, the social and ideological barriers that had kept women off the factory floor gave way. Women took on jobs as riveters, assemblers, and machinists, building bombers and tanks by day and tended their victory gardens by night.

A new study by two University of Michigan researchers, published in the *American Economic Review*, documents the dramatic rise in the number of women working in factories during this period. According to Sherrie A. Kossoudji and Laura J. Dresser, there were never more than 45 women working at Ford's massive River Rouge complex prior to the war. But as the war escalated and women were called in to replace men sent to the front, women suddenly accounted for 12% of the 93,000-member work force.

Their tenure in the plant was short, however. By war's end, women made up less than 1% of all hourly factory employees. As Kossoudji and Dresser explain, "Women were laid off from industrial firms disproportionately, and women with seniority rights were not recalled, nor were new women hired when postwar auto production expansion was associated with new hiring." To justify laying the women off and hiring male replacements, Ford managers claimed that the production process had altered so completely after the war that the occupations where women had proved themselves no longer existed.

Bombers were riveted; cars would be welded. Therefore, it was possible for Ford managers to make a somewhat unconvincing argument that women were no longer qualified. They claimed that the new auto production would require heavy lifting, not necessary in building bombers. As one woman put it, "They hire men there, they say, to do the heavy work. The women do light work. During the war, they didn't care what kind of work we did. . . ."

But after the war, they sure did. Kossoudji and Dresser conclude that, even when the jobs remained exactly the same, the ability of women to do them suddenly became suspect as the men returned from the front. "These women had, during the war, many of the exact jobs that became men's jobs after the war, using the same machines and drills. . . ." Even though the women had proven themselves capable workers, often more efficient than the men who had preceded them, the prejudice persisted that these were "men's" jobs. The brief time that women had spent in these jobs was not enough to change our cultural perception of factory work from "men's" work to "women's" work.

As such, Rosie was done in not by the men who came home from the front, nor by the men who ran the plant. Rosie was a victim of the power of definition, a demon that managerial women still struggle with today. For deeply embedded in our definition of what it means to be a manager is the belief that the manager will be male. In fact, being male and being a manager have been synonymous since the inception of the managerial class in the early 1900s.

If Men Are Good Managers, What Are Women?

As Rosabeth Moss Kanter explains in her ground-breaking work, *Men and Women of the Corporation*, professional managers succeeded in wresting control of the organization from its owners only by establishing their "expertise" in the "scientific" methods of management. This expertise was rooted in the characteristics our society has traditionally labeled "masculine": a tough-minded approach to problems; analytic abilities to abstract and plan; a capacity to set aside personal and emotional considerations in the interest of task accomplishment; and a cognitive superiority in problem solving and decision making. As Kanter reminds us, "These characteristics supposedly belonged only to men."

Women, on the other hand, historically have been viewed as having characteristics that were antithetical to modern management. They were "unfit" for the managerial role because they were "too emotional" and lacked the analytic abilities of men schooled in the scientific approach to management.

This link between masculine traits and managerial abilities had become well embedded in our organizational psyches by the middle of this century. A study published in the *Harvard Business Review* in 1965 entitled "Are Women Executives People?" reported that 32% of the respondents believed that a woman's fundamental biological makeup makes her unfit for a managerial role.

As recently as the mid-1970s, researchers found that the traits most commonly associated with being male continue to be synonymous with the traits managers are expected to exhibit. In "If 'Good Managers' Are Masculine, What Are 'Bad Managers'?" from the journal *Sex Roles*, Gary N. Powell and D. Anthony Butterfield report that the traditionally "masculine" characteristics of self-reliance, independence, aggression, and dominance have become inseparable from our defini-tion of managers. Their poll of 1,368 business students of both sexes revealed that between 67% to 85% describe a good manager as pos-sessing these so-called "masculine" traits. It was this belief that men were made for the job that greeted women managers when they first joined corporations in large numbers in the mid-1970s, and it has plagued them ever since.

The Metamorphosis of the Managerial Woman

Not surprisingly, the first women managers attempted to fit them-selves into the managerial role by adopting a "masculine" style. They dressed like men, they talked like men, they even tried to use sports analogies as men did.

In her best-seller, *Games Mother Never Taught You*, Betty Lehan Har-ragan argues that, in order to succeed as managers, women need to understand the elaborate sports metaphor after which business is pat-terned. She asserts that "management patterns its functions after the most sophisticated of all team games—football," then goes on to coach women on the intricacies of the game. "If you recover a fumble, complete a long pass, or make a long run into scoring position, press your advantage and capitalize on your opportunity to confound the opponents; try a trick play on the next down."

Unfortunately, as Rosie had already proved, it isn't easy for women to fit themselves into a male model. Women would have to under-stand more than fourth-down plays to be successful in business. After a decade of failing with the football paradigm and an equal number of years wearing bad clothes, women began to realize that it was impos-sible to disguise their essential nature in the workplace. Most obvi-ously, it was impossible to ignore pregnancy and motherhood and their impact on a manager's worklife. So it was that in the late 1980s the "Mommy Track" was born.

In "Management Women and the New Facts of Life," published in *Harvard Business Review* in 1989, Felice N. Schwartz wrote, "The one immutable, enduring difference between men and women is mater-nity." As such, Schwartz points out, pregnancy remains one issue where "female socialization" comes face-to-face with a male corporate culture. Male executives "place every working woman on a contin-uum that runs from total dedication to career at one end to a balance between career and family at the other. What women discover is that the male corporate culture sees both extremes as unacceptable. Women who want the flexibility to balance their families and their careers are not adequately committed to the organization. Women who perform as aggressively and competitively as men are abrasive and unfeminine." Not to mention bad mothers.

Part of Schwartz's solution to this dilemma is to separate women into two groups: "career primary" and "career and family" women. The corporation then can channel women onto different tracks: the fast track or what the *New York Times* later dubbed the "Mommy Track."

This simple suggestion started a heated national debate. On one side were critics who fervently believed that, since men were not being asked to choose between work and family, women shouldn't be asked to either. On the other side were those who sought to be "pragmatic" and argued that, since most women would leave the work force at some point to have children, it was logical to separate them out anyway. The debate ricocheted throughout the national media for several weeks before the concept was derailed altogether.

A Return to the Basics of Sexual Politics

More recently, it has been in vogue to argue that women, who allegedly possess special intuitive and caring abilities, actually make better managers than men, who are now hopelessly trapped into the outdated scientific paradigm of management. Recent publications have extolled the "special" capabilities of women managers, arguing that women have a unique ability to engage in the interactive forms of leadership that are needed in corporations today.

In *The Female Advantage*, Sally Helgesen writes, "As women's leadership qualities come to play a more dominant role in the public sphere, their particular aptitudes for long-term negotiating, analytic listening, and creating an ambiance in which people work with zest and spirit will help reconcile the split between the ideals of being efficient and being humane. This integration of female values is already producing a more collaborative kind of leadership, and changing the very ideal of what strong leadership actually is."

In this equation, women who were once thought to be inferior leaders because they were "too emotional" now turn out to be excellent leaders because they can exhibit "special" emotional qualities.

For authors like Helgesen, motherhood is no longer a liability; it is actually an advanced management training program. As one woman executive who is quoted in *The Female Advantage* says, "If you can figure out which one gets the gumdrop, the four-year-old or the six-year-old, you can negotiate any contract in the world."

In its way, this is as simplistic as the application of sports metaphors to management. Managers aren't mothers any more than they are quarterbacks. Both the sports metaphors and the new maternal metaphor of management are elaborate extensions of prevailing sexual stereotypes, the strong beliefs we hold about the way men and women should behave, translated into a business context.

Still, there exists a persistent notion that the special sensitivity of some women can lead us to a new kind of interactional leadership. For example, in "Ways Women Lead," [Chapter 2, Part I, this volume], Judy B. Rosener speaks glowingly about the work of a woman in an investment bank who "hosts dinners for her division, gives out gag gifts as party favors, passes out M&M's at meetings, and throws parties 'to celebrate ourselves.'"

Most likely, these women lack the organizational power necessary to create change and therefore fall back on the soft skills of nurturing and feeding people to gain allegiance. After all, women have been using food to cause groups to coalesce for years. By extolling this brand of manipulation, authors like Rosener are doing little more than making a virtue out of necessity.

And while there is much to be said for creating more humane work environments, and much debate over whether M&M's will do the trick, it is hard to imagine a book written for the male manager that suggests that what he needs to do to be successful is to bring cookies to meetings—unless, of course, he happens to be the Pillsbury Dough-boy.

Despite the popularity of the idea that women bring something special to the management table, there is also a certain danger inherent in this belief. For even as we seek to define gender roles, we perpetuate them. For it is the very definitions that authors like Helgesen suggest women cling to that have excluded women from managerial ranks in the past. The skills Helgesen claims will make women exemplary managers are the same skills Rosabeth Moss Kanter told us were the emotional characteristics that define the other—the lesser skills that sit beside the rational manager.

Women, therefore, have bought into and are currently promoting the very definitions that have been used to exclude them from the work force in the past. If women start to define themselves as good at the soft skills of communications, you better believe that someone will say that the "real" work of managers is number crunching and strategic analysis—things that women, well, just aren't up to. Remember, as soon as Rosie got good at riveting, factory work was all about welding.

The Double Bind

Adding to the complexity of this issue is one inescapable truth: women today cannot avoid being judged as women. As Rosabeth Moss Kanter warned, women are "often measured by two yardsticks: how *as women* they carried out the sales or management role; and how *as managers* they lived up to images of womanhood." By claiming that women bring "special" emotional and communications skills to the workplace, we damn the women who do not.

Take the case of Ann Hopkins, a woman who approached her job as a consultant by exhibiting a traditional male approach to authority. Hopkins was in her early forties in 1983 when she was denied a partnership at the accounting firm of Price Waterhouse. Even though she had generated more business and billed more hours than any other candidate up for partnership at the time, her application was rejected. When she discussed her rejection with the firm's chairman, Joseph Connor, Hopkins was told to relax and "take charge less often." Another partner suggested that she try to appear more feminine and wear more jewelry and makeup. Ann Hopkins had succeeded at being an accountant, but she had failed, in their eyes anyway, at being a woman.

This double yardstick of gender appropriateness and managerial effectiveness often leaves women in an unbreakable, untenable double bind. Women who attempt to fit themselves into a managerial role by acting like men, as Ann Hopkins did, are forced to behave in a sexually dissonant way. They risk being characterized as "too aggressive," or worse, just plain "bitchy." Yet women who act like ladies, speaking indirectly and showing concern for others, risk being seen as "ineffective," as someone skilled in the soft side of communications but unable to do the hard work of management.

After looking at a large number of sex discrimination cases, Deborah L. Rhode, a law professor at Stanford University, found that women have been denied promotions both for being ambitious and argumentative and for being old-fashioned and reserved. In other words, she found that there is often no acceptable way to bridge the gap between womanhood and work. And no way to break the bind that keeps women out of the top ranks of corporations.

If the norm is male, women will always be the other, the deviant. Superior or inferior, she is not the same. She is caught in a catch-22. If she attacks the problem by trying to be male, she will be too aggressive. If she attacks the problem by trying to be female, she will be the ineffective other.

Day to day, this translates into a minefield for women who must manage both their sexuality and their managerial performance. A recent study published in the *Journal of Personality and Social Psychology* shows that women who communicate indirectly or "nicely" are more effective than women who do not. In other words, women whose behavior is consistent with our cultural expectations of femininity are more successful than women who choose to behave in an "un-feminine" way. For example, women who use disclaimers such as "I'm no expert," "I don't know," and "I mean" and phrases such as "kind of," "sort of," and "you know" have a greater chance of influencing men than women who are more direct in their speech. Even though the women who use these phrases run the risk of undermining their message.

To come to this conclusion, Holy Cross Professor Linda L. Carli asked 229 undergraduates to rate female and male speakers on persuasive ability. She found that "men were influenced to a greater degree by women who speak tentatively than by those who speak assertively." She concludes, "It may be important for a woman not to behave too competitively or assertively when interacting with men in order for her to wield any influence, even if she may risk appearing incompetent."

To make matters worse, a woman will actually hurt her credibility with women colleagues when she uses the "indirect" style that works with men. Ask any woman who has ever tried to navigate this cultural and linguistic minefield, and she will tell you that it is next to impossible. Indeed, a growing number of researchers are pointing to this complex set of contradicting gender and managerial expectations as the chief nemesis of women in the work world. At the very least, the need to first and foremost manage their sexuality puts an extra burden on women already carrying a heavy load and trying to compete as managers.

As Rosie proved, what matters most is the ability to get the job done. What matters least is whether a man or a woman is doing it. Yet, ironically, that is what we have come to focus on.

A Way Out

Rosabeth Moss Kanter in *Men and Women of the Corporation* put forth the hopeful hypothesis that sheer numbers of women in the work force could overcome this problem. Once a critical mass of women had been achieved in any organization, she surmised, people would stop seeing them as women and evaluate their work as managers. Unfortunately, and only with the benefit of hindsight, is it possible to say that this hopeful hypothesis has not been borne out. Large numbers of women are clustered at entry-level and mid-level positions in both the professions and the corporations, and still women have not reached the top nor broken many of the sexual stereotypes that hold them back.

New research conducted at Harvard's John F. Kennedy School of Government by Robin J. Ely shows that it will take more than a critical mass of women at mid-level to eliminate women's token status in the work world. The key to changing the way women are perceived in any organization will be a critical mass of women at the senior levels. Ely states that "until women receive adequate representation at the top levels of the organization, sex role stereotypes will persist, largely to the detriment of women, as the basis for women's *own* sense of how they differ from men and as the basis for their *own* sense of their individual and collective value to their organizations."

After studying eight law firms, Ely's surprising finding is that not only do men view women differently when there is a critical mass of female senior executives in an organization, but women also view themselves differently. For example, Ely reports that women in firms with few senior women are less serious about their work, less satisfied with their firms, less self-confident, and less interested in promotion compared with women in firms with significant numbers of women in senior positions. Ely concludes that this "may account for the disturbing rate of turnover among talented women many organizations are facing today."

Which, of course, presents us with a sort of Gordian knot. If the only way to get more women to the top of corporations is to have more women at the top of corporations, we are left with a riddle, not a breakthrough.

Unless we remember what Rosie taught us. Rosie was suddenly able to "man" the war-making machine because the whole country was in a crisis, a crisis not so radically different from the competitive crisis we are all facing today.

It is often possible during times of crisis to overlook gender identification and look simply for those who can do the job. Surely, if women can be middle managers, then women can be senior managers. The key is not seeing them as women. The key is to focus on their abilities to perform the job at hand.

We know that effective leaders use both the more traditional, male, authoritarian style and the new, feminine, interactive style. Women must be allowed to use both as well, without confronting or confounding some rigid sexual stereotype.

If Rosie can rivet, she certainly can weld. If thousands of women managers can be effective at mid-levels of the corporation, surely some can cut it at the top. The key is to evaluate those near the top based on results, not on whether they've ever been mothers or plan not to be mothers. Not on whether they dress well or poorly. The key question is, can they do the job? And even more important, can they be taught to do the job? After all, a woman who can rivet can learn to weld. As Rosie once said, "We can do it!"

2
Ways Women Lead

Judy B. Rosener

Women managers who have broken the glass ceiling in medium-sized, nontraditional organizations have proven that effective leaders don't come from one mold. They have demonstrated that using the command-and-control style of managing others, a style generally associated with men in large, traditional organizations, is not the only way to succeed.

The first female executives, because they were breaking new ground, adhered to many of the "rules of conduct" that spelled success for men. Now a second wave of women is making its way into top management, not by adopting the style and habits that have proved successful for men but by drawing on the skills and attitudes they developed from their shared experience as women. These second-generation managerial women are drawing on what is unique to their socialization as women and creating a different path to the top. They are seeking and finding opportunities in fast-changing and growing organizations to show that they can achieve results—in a different way. They are succeeding because of—not in spite of—certain characteristics generally considered to be "feminine" and inappropriate in leaders.

The women's success shows that a nontraditional leadership style is well suited to the conditions of some work environments and can increase an organization's chances of surviving in an uncertain world. It supports the belief that there is strength in a diversity of leadership styles.

In a recent survey sponsored by the International Women's Forum,

I found a number of unexpected similarities between men and women leaders along with some important differences. Among these similarities are characteristics related to money and children. I found that the men and women respondents earned the same amount of money (and the household income of the women is twice that of the men). This finding is contrary to most studies, which find a considerable wage gap between men and women, even at the executive level. I also found that just as many men as women experience work-family conflict (although when there are children at home, the women experience slightly more conflict than men).

But the similarities end when men and women describe their leadership performance and how they usually influence those with whom they work. The men are more likely than the women to describe themselves in ways that characterize what some management experts call "transactional" leadership.[1] That is, they view job performance as a series of transactions with subordinates—exchanging rewards for services rendered or punishment for inadequate performance. The men are also more likely to use power that comes from their organizational position and formal authority.

The women respondents, on the other hand, described themselves in ways that characterize "transformational" leadership—getting subordinates to transform their own self-interest into the interest of the group through concern for a broader goal. Moreover, they ascribe their power to personal characteristics like charisma, interpersonal skills, hard work, or personal contacts rather than to organizational stature.

Intrigued by these differences, I interviewed some of the women respondents who described themselves as transformational. These discussions gave me a better picture of how these women view themselves as leaders and a greater understanding of the important ways in which their leadership style differs from the traditional command-and-control style. I call their leadership style "interactive leadership" because these women actively work to make their interactions with subordinates positive for everyone involved. More specifically, the women encourage participation, share power and information, enhance other people's self-worth, and get others excited about their work. All these things reflect their belief that allowing employees to contribute and to feel powerful and important is a win-win situation—good for the employees and the organization.

Interactive Leadership

From my discussions with the women interviewees, several patterns emerged. The women leaders made frequent reference to their efforts to encourage participation and share power and information—two things that are often associated with participative management. But their self-description went beyond the usual definitions of participation. Much of what they described were attempts to enhance other people's sense of self-worth and to energize followers. In general, these leaders believe that people perform best when they feel good about themselves and their work, and they try to create situations that contribute to that feeling.

Encourage participation. Inclusion is at the core of interactive leadership. In describing nearly every aspect of management, the women interviewees made reference to trying to make people feel part of the organization. They try to instill this group identity in a variety of ways, including encouraging others to have a say in almost every aspect of work, from setting performance goals to determining strategy. To facilitate inclusion, they create mechanisms that get people to participate and they use a conversational style that sends signals inviting people to get involved.

One example of the kinds of mechanisms that encourage participation is the "bridge club" that one interviewee, a group executive in charge of mergers and acquisitions at a large East Coast financial firm, created. The club is an informal gathering of people who have information she needs but over whom she has no direct control. The word *bridge* describes the effort to bring together these "members" from different functions. The word *club* captures the relaxed atmosphere.

Despite the fact that attendance at club meetings is voluntary and over and above the usual work demands, the interviewee said that those whose help she needs make the time to come. "They know their contributions are valued, and they appreciate the chance to exchange information across functional boundaries in an informal setting that's fun." She finds participation in the club more effective than memos.

Whether or not the women create special forums for people to interact, they try to make people feel included as a matter of course, often by trying to draw them into the conversation or soliciting their opinions. Frieda Caplan, founder and CEO of Frieda's Finest, a California-based marketer and distributor of unusual fruits and vegetables, described an approach she uses that is typical of the other women interviewed: "When I face a tough decision, I always ask my employees, 'What would you do if you were me?' This approach generates good ideas and introduces my employees to the complexity of management decisions."

Of course, saying that you include others doesn't mean others necessarily feel included. The women acknowledge the possibility that their efforts to draw people in may be seen as symbolic, so they try to avoid that perception by acting on the input they receive. They ask for suggestions before they reach their own conclusions, and they test— and sometimes change—particular decisions before they implement them. These women use participation to clarify their own views by thinking things through out loud and to ensure that they haven't overlooked an important consideration.

The fact that many of the interviewees described their participatory style as coming "naturally" suggests that these leaders do not consciously adopt it for its business value. Yet they realize that encouraging participation has benefits. For one thing, making it easy for people to express their ideas helps ensure that decisions reflect as much information as possible. To some of the women, this point is just common sense. Susan S. Elliott, president and founder of Systems Service Enterprises, a St. Louis computer consulting company, expressed this view: "I can't come up with a plan and then ask those who manage the accounts to give me their reactions. They're the ones who really know the accounts. They have information I don't have. Without their input I'd be operating in an ivory tower."

Participation also increases support for decisions ultimately reached and reduces the risk that ideas will be undermined by unexpected opposition. Claire Rothman, general manager of the Great Western Forum, a large sports and entertainment arena in Los Angeles, spoke about the value of open disagreement: "When I know ahead of time that someone disagrees with a decision, I can work especially closely with that person to try to get his or her support."

Getting people involved also reduces the risk associated with having only one person handle a client, project, or investment. For Patricia M. Cloherty, senior vice president and general partner of Alan Patricof Associates, a New York venture capital firm, including people in decision making and planning gives investments longevity. If something happens to one person, others will be familiar enough with the situation to "adopt" the investment. That way, there are no orphans in the portfolio, and a knowledgeable second opinion is always available.

Like most who are familiar with participatory management, these women are aware that being inclusive also has its disadvantages. Soliciting ideas and information from others takes time, often requires giving up some control, opens the door to criticism, and exposes personal and turf conflicts. In addition, asking for ideas and information can be interpreted as not having answers.

Further, it cannot be assumed that everyone wants to participate. Some people prefer being told what to do. When Mary Jane Rynd was a partner in a Big Eight accounting firm in Arizona (she recently left to start her own company—Rynd, Carneal & Associates), she encountered such a person: "We hired this person from an out-of-state CPA firm because he was experienced and smart—and because it's always fun to hire someone away from another firm. But he was just too cynical to participate. He was suspicious of everybody. I tried everything to get him involved—including him in discussions and giving him pep talks about how we all work together. Nothing worked. He just didn't want to participate."

Like all those who responded to the survey, these women are comfortable using a variety of leadership styles. So when participation doesn't work, they act unilaterally. "I prefer participation," said Elliott, "but there are situations where time is short and I have to take the bull by the horns."

Share power and information. Soliciting input from other people suggests a flow of information from employees to the "boss." But part of making people feel included is knowing that open communication flows in two directions. These women say they willingly share power and information rather than guard it and they make apparent their reasoning behind decisions. While many leaders see information as power and power as a limited commodity to be coveted, the interviewees seem to be comfortable letting power and information change hands. As Adrienne Hall, vice chairman of Eisaman, Johns & Laws, a large West Coast advertising firm, said: "I know territories shift, so I'm not preoccupied with turf."

One example of power and information sharing is the open strategy sessions held by Debi Coleman, vice president of information systems and technology at Apple Computer. Rather than closeting a small group of key executives in her office to develop a strategy based on her own agenda, she holds a series of meetings over several days and allows a larger group to develop and help choose alternatives.

The interviewees believe that sharing power and information accomplishes several things. It creates loyalty by signaling to coworkers and subordinates that they are trusted and their ideas respected. It also sets an example for other people and therefore can enhance the general communication flow. And it increases the odds that leaders will hear about problems before they explode. Sharing power and information also gives employees and coworkers the wherewithal to reach conclusions, solve problems, and see the justification for decisions.

On a more pragmatic level, many employees have come to expect their bosses to be open and frank. They no longer accept being dictated to but want to be treated as individuals with minds of their own. As Elliott said, "I work with lots of people who are bright and intelligent, so I have to deal with them at an intellectual level. They're very logical, and they want to know the reasons for things. They'll buy in only if it makes sense."

In some cases, sharing information means simply being candid about work-related issues. In early 1990, when Elliott hired as employees many of the people she had been using as independent contractors, she knew the transition would be difficult for everyone. The number of employees nearly doubled overnight, and the nature of working relationships changed. "I warned everyone that we were in for some rough times and reminded them that we would be experiencing them together. I admitted that it would also be hard for me, and I made it clear that I wanted them to feel free to talk to me. I was completely candid and encouraged them to be honest with me. I lost some employees who didn't like the new relationships, but I'm convinced that being open helped me understand my employees better, and it gave them a feeling of support."

Like encouraging participation, sharing power and information has its risks. It allows for the possibility that people will reject, criticize, or otherwise challenge what the leader has to say or, more broadly, her authority. Also, employees get frustrated when leaders listen to—but ultimately reject—their ideas. Because information is a source of power, leaders who share it can be seen as naive or needing to be liked. The interviewees have experienced some of these downsides but find the positives overwhelming.

Enhance the self-worth of others. One of the byproducts of sharing information and encouraging participation is that employees feel important. During the interviews, the women leaders discussed other ways they build a feeling of self-worth in coworkers and subordinates. They talked about giving others credit and praise and sending small signals of recognition. Most important, they expressed how they refrain from asserting their own superiority, which asserts the inferiority of others. All those I interviewed expressed clear aversion to behavior that sets them apart from others in the company—reserved parking places, separate dining facilities, pulling rank.

Examples of sharing and giving credit to others abound. Caplan, who has been the subject of scores of media reports hailing her innovation of labeling vegetables so consumers know what they are and how to cook them, originally got the idea from a farmer. She said that whenever someone raises the subject, she credits the farmer and downplays her role. Rothman is among the many note-writers: when someone does something out of the ordinary, she writes them a personal note to tell them she noticed. Like many of the women I interviewed, she said she also makes a point of acknowledging good work by talking about it in front of others.

Bolstering coworkers and subordinates is especially important in businesses and jobs that tend to be hard on a person's ego. Investment banking is one example because of the long hours, high pressures, intense competition, and inevitability that some deals will fail. One interviewee in investment banking hosts dinners for her division, gives out gag gifts as party favors, passes out M&Ms at meetings, and throws parties "to celebrate ourselves." These things, she said, balance the anxiety that permeates the environment.

Rynd compensates for the negativity inherent in preparing tax returns: "In my business we have something called a query sheet, where the person who reviews the tax return writes down everything that needs to be corrected. Criticism is built into the system. But at the end of every review, I always include a positive comment—your work paper technique looked good, I appreciate the fact that you got this done on time, or something like that. It seems trivial, but it's one way to remind people that I recognize their good work and not just their shortcomings."

Energize others. The women leaders spoke of their enthusiasm for work and how they spread their enthusiasm around to make work a challenge that is exhilarating and fun. The women leaders talked about it in those terms and claimed to use their enthusiasm to get others excited. As Rothman said, "There is rarely a person I can't motivate."

Enthusiasm was a dominant theme throughout the interviews. In computer consulting: "Because this business is on the forefront of technology, I'm sort of evangelistic about it, and I want other people to be as excited as I am." In venture capital: "You have to have a head of steam." In executive search: "Getting people excited is an important way to influence those you have no control over." Or in managing sports arenas: "My enthusiasm gets others excited. I infuse them with energy and make them see that even boring jobs contribute to the fun of working in a celebrity business."

Enthusiasm can sometimes be misunderstood. In conservative professions like investment banking, such an upbeat leadership style can be interpreted as cheerleading and can undermine credibility. In many cases, the women said they won and preserved their credibility by achieving results that could be measured easily. One of the women acknowledged that her colleagues don't understand or like her leadership style and have called it cheerleading. "But," she added, "in this business you get credibility from what you produce, and they love the profits I generate." While energy and enthusiasm can inspire some, it doesn't work for everyone. Even Rothman conceded, "Not everyone has a flame that can be lit."

Paths of Least Resistance

Many of the women I interviewed said the behaviors and beliefs that underlie their leadership style come naturally to them. I attribute this to two things: their socialization and the career paths they have chosen. Although socialization patterns and career paths are changing, the average age of the men and women who responded to the survey is 51—old enough to have had experiences that differed *because* of gender.

Until the 1960s, men and women received different signals about what was expected of them. To summarize a subject that many experts have explored in depth, women have been expected to be wives, mothers, community volunteers, teachers, and nurses. In all these roles, they are supposed to be cooperative, supportive, understanding, gentle, and to provide service to others. They are to derive satisfaction and a sense of self-esteem from helping others, including their spouses. While men have had to appear to be competitive, strong, tough, decisive, and in control, women have been allowed to be cooperative, emotional, supportive, and vulnerable. This may explain why women today are more likely than men to be interactive leaders.

Men and women have also had different career opportunities. Women were not expected to have careers, or at least not the same kinds of careers as men, so they either pursued different jobs or were simply denied opportunities men had. Women's career tracks have usually not included long series of organizational positions with formal authority and control of resources. Many women had their first work experiences outside the home as volunteers. While some of the challenges they faced as managers in volunteer organizations are the same as those in any business, in many ways, leading volunteers is different because of the absence of concrete rewards like pay and promotion.

As women entered the business world, they tended to find themselves in positions consistent with the roles they played at home: in staff positions rather than in line positions, supporting the work of others, and in functions like communications or human resources where they had relatively small budgets and few people reporting directly to them.

The fact that most women have lacked formal authority over others and control over resources means that by default they have had to find other ways to accomplish their work. As it turns out, the behaviors that were natural and/or socially acceptable for them have been highly successful in at least some managerial settings.

What came easily to women turned out to be a survival tactic. Although leaders often begin their careers doing what comes naturally and what fits within the constraints of the job, they also develop their skills and styles over time. The women's use of interactive leadership has its roots in socialization, and the women interviewees firmly believe that it benefits their organizations. Through the course of their careers, they have gained conviction that their style is effective. In fact, for some, it was their own success that caused them to formulate their philosophies about what motivates people, how to make good decisions, and what it takes to maximize business performance.

They now have formal authority and control over vast resources, but still they see sharing power and information as an asset rather than a liability. They believe that although pay and promotion are necessary tools of management, what people really want is to feel that they are contributing to a higher purpose and that they have the opportunity as individuals to learn and grow. The women believe that employees and peers perform better when they feel they are part of an organization and can share in its success. Allowing them to get involved and to work to their potential is a way of maximizing their contributions and using human resources most efficiently.

Another Kind of Diversity

The IWF survey shows that a nontraditional leadership style can be effective in organizations that accept it. This lesson comes especially hard to those who think of the corporate world as a game of survival of the fittest, where the fittest is always the strongest, toughest, most decisive, and powerful. Such a workplace seems to favor leaders who control people by controlling resources, and by controlling people, gain control of more resources. Asking for information and sharing decision-making power can be seen as serious disadvantages, but what is a disadvantage under one set of circumstances is an advantage under another. The "best" leadership style depends on the organizational context.

Only one of the women interviewees is in a traditional, large-scale company. More typically, the women's organizations are medium-sized and tend to have experienced fast growth and fast change. They demand performance and/or have a high proportion of professional workers. These organizations seem to create opportunities for women and are hospitable to those who use a nontraditional management style.

The degree of growth or change in an organization is an important factor in creating opportunities for women. When change is rampant, everything is up for grabs, and crises are frequent. Crises are generally not desirable, but they do create opportunities for people to prove themselves. Many of the women interviewees said they got their first break because their organizations were in turmoil.

Fast-changing environments also play havoc with tradition. Coming up through the ranks and being part of an established network is no longer important. What is important is how you perform. Also, managers in such environments are open to new solutions, new structures, and new ways of leading.

The fact that many of the women respondents are in organizations that have clear performance standards suggests that they have gained credibility and legitimacy by achieving results. In investment banking, venture capital, accounting, and executive placement, for instance, individual performance is easy to measure.

A high proportion of young professional workers—increasingly typical of organizations—is also a factor in some women's success. Young, educated professionals impose special requirements on their organizations. They demand to participate and contribute. In some cases, they have knowledge or talents their bosses don't have. If they are good performers, they have many employment options. It is easy to imagine that these professionals will respond to leaders who are inclusive and open, who enhance the self-worth of others, and who create a fun work environment. Interactive leaders are likely to win the cooperation needed to achieve their goals.

Interactive leadership has proved to be effective, perhaps even advantageous, in organizations in which the women I interviewed have succeeded. As the work force increasingly demands participation and the economic environment increasingly requires rapid change, interactive leadership may emerge as the management style of choice for many organizations. For interactive leadership to take root more broadly, however, organizations must be willing to question the notion that the traditional command-and-control leadership style that has brought success in earlier decades is the only way to get results. This may be hard in some organizations, especially those with long histories of male-oriented, command-and-control leadership. Changing these organizations will not be easy. The fact that women are more likely than men to be interactive leaders raises the risk that these companies will perceive interactive leadership as "feminine" and automatically resist it.

Linking interactive leadership directly to being female is a mistake. We know that women are capable of making their way through corporations by adhering to the traditional corporate model and that they can wield power in ways similar to men. Indeed, some women may prefer that style. We also know from the survey findings that some men use the transformational leadership style.

Large, established organizations should expand their definition of effective leadership. If they were to do that, several things might happen, including the disappearance of the glass ceiling and the creation of a wider path for all sorts of executives—men and women—to attain positions of leadership. Widening the path will free potential leaders to lead in ways that play to their individual strengths. Then the newly recognized interactive leadership style can be valued and rewarded as highly as the command-and-control style has been for decades. By valuing a diversity of leadership styles, organizations will find the strength and flexibility to survive in a highly competitive, increasingly diverse economic environment.

Note

1. Transactional and transformational leadership were first conceptualized by James McGregor Burns in *Leadership* (New York: Harper & Row, 1978) and later developed by Bernard Bass in *Leadership and Performance Beyond Expectations* (New York: Free Press, 1985).

3
Two Women, Three Men on a Raft

Robert Schrank

The day was cold and gray. Under the pines that towered over their heads, 20 people assembled on the banks of the Rogue River in Oregon. They were members of a special group invited by Outward Bound to take a trip down the river on a raft. There would be five rafts, each holding four participants and one Outward Bound staff member. Raft No. 4 was the only one that had two women and three men. When the trip started, all that the participants knew was that there would be rapids with fearsome names; that each was responsible for doing his or her share of the cooking, tent pitching, ground clearing, supply hauling, and paddling; and that their teamwork or lack of it was what would make their trip a success or a failure. They knew nothing of each other, their Outward Bound staff member, or what a week on the river could really be like. This is one participant's story of how Raft No. 4 fared on the Rogue and what the experience taught him about the relationships between men and women at work.

One afternoon in June, I left the cloistered halls of the Ford Foundation and within 36 hours found myself standing on the pebbled banks of the Rogue River in Oregon with three other uncertain souls who had embarked on a week of "survival training" sponsored by Outward Bound. It was a cloudy, cold day, and as we pumped up our rubber raft and contemplated the Rogue, we also wondered about each other.

Before embarking on a Greyhound for the raft launching site, we had gathered the night before at the Medford Holiday Inn. That night, the Outward Bound staff had distributed individual camping gear and waterproof sleeping/storage bags to the 20 of us, almost all novices, and had given us a short briefing on the perils of going down the Rogue River on a raft.

As they explained the nature of the trip, the Outward Bound staffers reminded me of seasoned military men or safari leaders about to take a group of know-nothings into a world of lurking danger. Their talk was a kind of machismo jargon about "swells," rattlers, safety lines, portages, and pitons. Because they had known and conquered the dangers, it seemed they could talk of such things with assurance. This kind of "man talk" called to a primitive ear in us novices, and we began to perceive the grave dangers out there as evils to be overcome. In our minds, we planned to meet "Big Foot" the very next day, and we were secretly thrilled at the prospect.

If the Outward Bound staff briefing was designed to put us at ease, its effect, if anything, was the opposite. Hearing the detailed outline of what would be expected of us increased our anxiety. "You will work in teams as assigned to your raft," said Bill Boyd, the Northwest Outward Bound director, "and you will be responsible for running your raft, setting up camp each night, cooking every fourth meal for the whole gang, and taking care of all your personal needs."

The staff divided the 20 of us into four groups, each of which would remain together for the week on the raft. How we were grouped was never explained, but of the five rafts on the river, No. 4 was the only one that ended up with two women and three men. One of the men was a member of the Outward Bound staff, a counselor and guide who was considerably younger than his four charges.

The four of us on Raft No. 4 were all in our middle fifties. Each of us had experienced some modicum of success in his or her life, and Outward Bound had invited each of us in the hope that after a week of living on the Rogue River we would go back from that trip as Outward Bound supporters and promoters.

Outward Bound exists because of the surprising fact that during World War II fewer younger men survived being torpedoed on the Murmansk, Russia convoy run than older men. Dr. Kurt Hahn, C.B.E., an emigrant German educator living in England, had observed that the older men did things to help themselves survive, such as collecting rain water for drinking, building shelters in the lifeboats, catching and eating raw fish, and learning to care for each other.

Dr. Hahn found that many of the younger seamen, by contrast, tended to sit and wait for somebody to come and rescue them. If no one came, which was often the case, they died just sitting there. Dr.

Hahn felt that these seamen must have lacked a certain self-confidence or an awareness that they could take action that would result in survival, and founded Outward Bound to help young people learn that they can take charge of their own survival and lives.

The worldwide organization has been operating in the United States for 14 years; its 35,000 graduates attest to its popularity. During this time, however, Outward Bound has evolved into more of a learning institution than a survival training organization. It now operates under a variety of different notions, one of them being that industrial man has lost and should regain the art of living with nature. The organization believes that the wilderness can teach people about themselves by providing a different backdrop against which they can gain insight into their day-to-day behavior.

This article is about what happened to two women and three men on a raft for a week on the Rogue River in Oregon.

On the River

Like most of the other 19 people on the trip, at the outset I had little or no idea of what to expect. I had participated in a few human growth encounter workshops, so I was prepared for, although again surprised at, how willingly people seem to accept the authority of a completely unknown group leader. Most people seem able to participate in all kinds of strange and, in many instances, new behaviors with no knowledge regarding the possible outcomes. This group was no exception. All of us had some notion of Outward Bound, but we knew nothing about each other, or our raft leader John, or the Rogue River.

Even though their preembarkation talk was filled with the machismo jargon I mentioned, the staff did not describe what we might actually expect to happen, nor did they talk about the many other river trips they had been on. I suppose the staff leaders assumed that the best way for a group of people to learn about themselves and each other is to let the experience talk to them directly.

The two women assigned to Raft No. 4 were named Marlene and Helen. Marlene was a recently divorced mother of five kids from Washington, whom a number of us had observed in her pink bikini in the Holiday Inn pool when we had arrived. Most of us acknowledged that because of that build we would love to have her along. Marlene used to wear her red ski suit at night and talked a lot about times she'd spent on the slopes. A top-notch skier, she said she divorced her husband because she was tired of making believe he was a better skier than she was.

Helen, a big blonde woman with a fierce sense of humor and a divorced mother of two grown boys, was at the time of our trip the president of the Fund Center in Denver, a coordinating body for local foundations, as well as a political activist. She and I became each other's clowns, and one night at a campfire she leaned over and asked me, "Bobbie, is this just another plaything of the bored rich, or can we really learn something out here in this Godforsaken wilderness?" I told her I wasn't sure but we ought to give it a chance, which we did.

One of the two other men was Bill, a very successful lawyer from Darien, Connecticut. He was the only one of the four passengers who was still happily married, since I too was divorced. Bill was a busy executive, but he managed to find time for hiking, skiing, and fishing. While Outward Bound took care of all our food requirements and most of our medical needs, Raft No. 4 had its own supply officer in Bill. His backpack was organized like a Civil War surgeon's field kit. He had all his changes of clothing scheduled, and when it rained, his extra plastic rainjacket kept me dry since mine leaked like a sieve. Though he and Marlene were obviously attracted to each other from the start, it was clear from his "happy family" talk that nothing was going to change, and it didn't.

The other man was John Rhodes, our heavily mustached, vigorous leader, in his early thirties, who saw himself as a teacher, educator, and trainer. As a progressive educator, John was overdedicated to the notion that no one can learn from anyone else since learning is a singular, unique experience. At night John slept away from the rest of us under a very fancy Abercrombie and Fitch drop cloth which was made to be strung up in many different ways. Trying a new fancy pitch, John would say to Bill and me, "Be imaginative in how you pitch your tarpaulin." As we had nothing but pieces of plastic as tarpaulins, we would greet John's injunction with amused silence.

The men and women of Raft No. 4 were a warm, friendly, outgoing bunch, each of whom helped create a nice supportive atmosphere.

When we arrived at the river, each was anxious to pitch in and do his or her part. The staff distributed the rafts, each of which had a small foot pump, and Bill and I, with instruction from John, proceeded to inflate ours. It was one of our first chores, and we did it with a machismo fervor that suggested either previous knowledge, or that it was man's work, or both. Marlene and Helen carried food bags, buckets, and ropes. It was a cold day, a gray mist hung over the towering Oregon pines, and I had a feeling that at least some of us, given a choice, would have opted for going back to the Holiday Inn. There was a lot of forced joking and kidding, with which we attempted to overcome some of our anxieties—we were whistling in the dark.

John gave each of us a Mae West type life preserver and instructed us on how to use it. He told us, "You are not to go on the raft without it." Now with all of us bulging out of our Mae Wests, a Richter scale applied to anxiety would have registered eight or a full-scale breakdown. Postponing the inevitable, we shivered, fussed, and helped each other get adjusted to our life jackets. The trip down the Rogue was beginning to have a serious quality.

The rafts we used were small, about 10 feet long and 4 feet wide. The passengers sit on the inflated outer tube with their feet on the inside. Everyone is very close together with little or no room to move around. Also, unlike a boat, a raft has no keel or rudder mechanism, which means that it tends to roll and bobble around on top of the water. Unless the occupants work as a team and use their paddles in close coordination, it is very difficult to control.

While we were still on shore, John perched himself in the helmsman position at the back of the raft and said, "OK, I am going to teach you how to navigate the Rogue. When I say 'right turn,' the two people on the left side of the raft are to paddle forward and the two on the right are to backpaddle. When I say 'left turn,' the two people on the right are to paddle forward and the two on the left are to backpaddle. When I say 'forward,' I want everyone digging that paddle in like his life depended on it, and when I say 'backpaddle,' everyone paddle backward. When I say 'hold,' all paddles out of the water. Now you got it, or should we go over it again?" We pushed the raft out over the beach pebbles and paddled out into the Rogue, which at this point seemed like a nice pond. John barked his commands, and the team did just fine in the quiet water.

John told us that we were Raft No. 4 of five rafts, and it was important to everyone's safety that each raft maintain its position so that we could make periodic personnel checks to make sure no one was missing. John gave the command "forward," and because No. 3 raft was already far ahead of us and out of sight, Marlene, Helen, Bill, and I paddled vigorously.

As we proceeded down the river, John announced, "Each of you will take turns at being the helmsman." After some comment by Helen, this term was quickly corrected to conform to the new nondiscriminatory linguistics, as well as for the EEOC, to "helmsperson." John said that this person would be in charge of the raft—steering from the stern and issuing the commands.

As John talked, my mind drifted. I was suddenly overwhelmed by the grandeur and beauty of this great wilderness river road we were traveling. In awe of the hugeness of the trees, I did not hear nor respond to a command. John, a very earnest fellow, was somewhat annoyed at my daydreaming and upbraided me saying, "Look, we all have to concentrate on our job or we will be in trouble." And then he explained the nature of the rapids up ahead.

He told us how to recognize a rapid's tongue (entrance), how to avoid "sleepers" (hidden rocks), and then how to ride the "haystacks" (the choppy waves that form at the outlet of the rapids) as you come through the rapids. He said that the most important art we would learn would be how to chop our paddles into the waves as we rode the haystacks. Since a raft has no seat belts, or even seats for that matter, unless you chop down hard the rough water can bounce you right out of it.

As we paddled through the still calm waters, trying to catch up with Raft No. 3, Helen began to complain that she was already getting tired. "I'm just not used to pushing a paddle, but I'm damn good at pushing a pencil," she said. I too was beginning to feel the strain of the paddle, but rather than admit it, I just laughed saying, "Why this is nothing, Helen. You should canoe the St. John in Maine. That would teach you." Bill chimed in with "Yeah, this is nothing compared to climbing Pike's Peak."

As we moved down the river a faint distant roar broke the silence of the forest. And as we drew nearer to it, our excitement grew bigger. One might have thought that rather than a 4-foot rapids, Niagara Falls lay dead ahead. I was relieved when, some distance before the rapids, John told us to head for the bank where we would go ashore and study the rapids. As a team we would then decide what kind of a course to take through them.

We had been on the river now for a few hours, and, as it would be many times during the trip, getting on dry land was a great relief. Life on a small rubber raft consists of sitting in ankle-deep cold water, anticipating a periodic refill over both the side of the raft and one's genitals. If there was not time to bail out, we would just sit in the cold water. And even if there were time we would still be soaking wet and cold from the hips down. Though this was our first chance to escape the cold water treatment, we quickly learned to look forward to such opportunities. The physical discomfort we felt together on the raft was overcoming our sense of being strangers; by the time we disembarked that first time, we were a band of fellow sufferers.

At that point on the river, the bank was very steep, so we had a tough climb up a high rock cliff to get a good look at the rapids. Just before the rapids, the river makes a sharp 90-degree bend creating an additional danger. The swiftly running river could pile the raft up on the bank or into a hidden rock. After considerable discussion, during which Bill and I tried to demonstrate to Helen and Marlene our previous if not superior knowledge of boating, we agreed on taking a left course into the tongue while at the same time trying to bear right to avoid being swept onto the bank.

Coming up and down the steep river bank Bill helped Marlene over the rocks, holding her elbow. A ways behind them Helen commented to me, "Honestly, Bob, Marlene isn't that helpless." As we climbed into the raft, Bill helped Marlene again, and I, smiling sheepishly, offered my arm to Helen. I said, holding the raft, "Well, if we go, we all go together, and may we all end up in the same hospital room." Sitting herself down, Helen said, "Who will notify next of kin since no one will be left." After they were seated, Bill and I huddled and agreed that if anything went wrong, he would look after Marlene and I would look after Helen.

Once back on the river, with John at the helm, we paddled into the rapid's tongue, where the raft picked up speed. Staying to the left but maintaining our right orientation, before we knew what had happened, we were roaring through the tongue, roller coasting through the haystacks, screaming with excitement. Flushed with our first real achievement, the raft awash with ice-cold water, we patted each other on the back on our first great success. While bailing out the raft we paid each other compliments and convinced ourselves that we could master the Rogue River.

But this was our first set of rapids, and while John assured us that we had done well, he also reminded us of the meaner rapids yet to come with such potent names as Mule Creek Canyon, Blossom Bar, Big Bend, Copper Canyon, and Grave Creek. My God, I thought, did we really have to go through all of those terrible places?

Life on the Rogue included many other things besides shooting rapids. We pitched tarpaulins every night, lugged supplies in and out of the raft, and became accustomed to the discomforts of having no running water and of being absolutely frozen after sitting in cold water for a whole day. Nothing cements a group together like collective misery, and the people of Raft No. 4 had a *real* concern for each other as mutually suffering humans.

Each raft carried a watertight supply bag of sleeping bags and personal clothing. The bag was strapped to the front of the raft and had to be carried to and fro every morning and night. When we tied up at our first campsite, Marlene and Helen each took an end and started to carry the bag from the raft up the bank. Bill ran after them yelling, "Hey, hold it. That's too heavy for you," and grabbed the bag. Throwing it over his shoulder, he said, "You shouldn't try to do that heavy stuff." Marlene smiled and said, "Bill, anytime, be my guest." Helen, who was a little annoyed, commented sarcastically, "Well, it's great to have these big, strong men around now, ain't it though?"

When we came off the raft at night, most everybody instantly undressed to put on dry clothes, caring not one fig for a leaf or modesty. But even though on the surface it looked as though the physical sex differences had disappeared, the emergency nature of things exerted a different pressure, forcing each of us to "do what you know best."

Bill and I, for example, would pitch the tarpaulins each night and haul water, while Marlene and Helen would make the beds, clean the ground, and arrange the sleeping bags. Our mutual concern was evident, it was a beautiful experience of caring for one's fellow sisters and brothers, and I loved it.

After pitching our plastic tarpaulins (which were not much bigger than queen-size beds) as protection against the rain, the four of us would wiggle into our sleeping bags for the night. The first night Helen said she thought we were "four wonderful people gone batty sleeping on the hard cold ground when they could all be in soft feather beds." We laughed and helped each other zip up, arranged sweaters as pillows, and made sure we were all protected. Raft No. 4 was a real team.

During the days, I was beginning to learn some basics about rafts and rapids. Once the raft starts down the river and enters a swiftly moving rapid, the helmsperson must give and the crew respond to commands in quick succession in order to avoid hidden rocks, suck holes, boulders, and other obstacles, which can either flip the raft over or pull it under, bouncing it back like a ball.

As we approached the second rapids, we again went ashore to "look over our approach." It was a bad situation as the rapids planed out over a very rocky riverbed. Helen suggested that we let John take the raft through while we watch. "Now, Bob," she said, "do we really care about this damn river? I don't care if we can squeak through these rocks or not. Hit your head on them or something and you could really get hurt." Bill, John, and I cheered us on.

When I became helmsperson, I discovered quickly how difficult it is to steer a raft. The helmsperson can have some effect on the direction in which the raft goes, and because Bill and I had some boating experience, we were at least familiar with the idea of using the paddle as a rudder. Neither Helen nor Marlene seemed to understand how to use a paddle that way, nor did they have the experience.

When one of the two women on our raft, more so Marlene than Helen, was the helmsperson, she would chant, "I can't do it; I can't do it." Each time they cried out neither Bill nor I would answer right away, but we would eventually try to convince them that they could. Typically, Marlene would say, "I don't know right from left. One of you guys do it; you're so much better."

At Copper Canyon we needed a "hard right" command. With Marlene at the helm, we got a "hard left" instead. Bill and I looked at each other in utter disgust.

He asked Marlene, "What's the matter, honey?"

She said, "I don't know right from left. You be the helmsperson."

He said, "Why don't we write on the back of your hands 'right' and 'left'?"

Bill was kidding, but the next thing I knew, they were doing it.

Helen was mad and said to me, "Is it really necessary to make a baby out of her?"

"No," I said, "of course not. But she really doesn't know right from left."

As Marlene would say, "I can't do it" Bill and I would say, "Of course you can do it. It's easy; you're doing just fine." All the time we were speaking, we were thinking, "Ye gods! When is she going to give up?" Each time either Marlene or Helen would be helmsperson, we'd have the same conversation; each time Bill's and my reassurances would be more and more halfhearted. Before long we weren't responding at all.

As the days wore on, Bill and I proceeded subtly but surely to take charge. The teamwork was unraveling. When we approached a tongue, if either Marlene or Helen were helmsperson, Bill and I would look at each other, and with very slight headshakes and grimaces we would indicate agreement that things were not going well at all. Once we had established that things were not going well, we then felt free to take our own corrective measures, such as trying to steer the raft from our forward paddle positions, an almost impossible thing to do. Not only is running the raft from the front not at all helpful to the person at the helm, but also if the helmsperson is not aware of the counterforces, the raft can easily turn around like a carousel. The unaware helmsperson is then totally out of control. When that would happen, Marlene would say, "I just don't know what's wrong with me," and Helen would echo, "I don't know what's wrong with me either." Bill's and my disgust would mount.

Eventually, John became fed up with the inability of the bunch on Raft No. 4 to work together, which was mainly a result, he said, of the two "captains" in the front. As a last resort he ordered each one of us to give a single command that he or she would shout as needed. My command was "hold," Bill's command was "left," Marlene's was "right," and Helen's was "backpaddle." John's teaching objective was to get the four of us working together, or else. Needless to say, "or else" prevailed.

On the fifth day, Marlene was helmsperson. Bill and I were in the bow, silently anxious. Even voluble Helen was silent as the raft approached a fast-moving chute. At that time only a clear, concise, direct command and a rapid response would be of any use at all.

Instead of a "hard right" command, we had no command. Marlene froze, the raft slid up on a big boulder, and in an instant we flipped over like a flapjack on a griddle. The current was swift and swept the five of us away in different directions. As I splashed around in the cold water, cursing that "Goddamned dumb Marlene," I spotted Bill nearby. The two of us began together to look for Marlene and Helen, whom we found each grappling with paddles and gear they'd grabbed as the raft had gone over. We assured each other we were OK and expressed relief at finding each other.

Cold, wet, and shivering uncontrollably, we made our way out of the river. To warm us and to keep us moving, John chased us around the bank to get wood for a fire. He stuffed us with candies and other sweets to give us energy. As we stood around the fire, chilled and wet, unable to stop shaking, we talked about what had happened, and why.

There was mutiny in the air now and a consensus emerged. The four of us were furious at John and blamed him for our predicament. John retreated, but finally we were agreed that we would not have any more of this kind of thing. Regardless of John's wishes, anyone who did not want to be helmsperson could simply pass. Marlene was certain that she wanted no part of being at the helm, and Helen, though less sure, was happy to say, "Yeah, I just want to stay dry. Let you guys take the helm."

After becoming somewhat dry, sober, and a bit remorseful, the crew of Raft No. 4 returned to the river to resume our run down the Rogue. We had lost our No. 4 position, the other rafts having run past us. John was helmsperson. Helen and Marlene were settled into their backpaddle seats. Bill and I, miffed over our mishap, felt self-conscious and fell silent thinking of the inevitable joshing we'd receive from the other rafts.

We slowly overcame the tensions of our crisis, and as the trip came to an end, we were friends again; the fifth day was forgotten. As we climbed out of the raft for the last time, Marlene said, "Well, the next raft trip I take, it will be as a passenger and not as a crew member."

That last night on the Rogue, we celebrated with a big party. The women dressed up in improvised bangles and baubles. I was the maitre d', and none of us thought much about what really had happened on Raft No. 4.

Deliverance

What really happened on the river? Why did the raft flip over? Not until I was back in the comfort of my office did I begin to understand, and the realization of the truth was as shocking as any of the splashes of cold water had been on the Rogue. It became clear to me that not only had I been unhappy with a woman as helmsperson, but also that Bill and I had subconsciously, by habit, proceeded to undermine the women. When one of the other two men was in charge, I was comfortable, supportive, and worked to help him be a better helmsperson. When a woman was at the helm, I seemed to direct my activity at getting her replaced rapidly by one of the men.

A most revealing part of the raft experience, however, was not so much the power relationship between the sexes, which I think I understood, but how Bill and I unconsciously or automatically responded to protect our power from female encroachment. When the trip started, I knew that I might have some difficulty accepting a woman at the helm, but I did not realize that the threat would be so great that I would actually desire to see her fail. On that trip I did something new: I actively tried to sabotage Marlene's and Helen's efforts to lead.

Bill and I were unconsciously building on each woman's doubts about herself with negative reinforcement of her leadership role. The effect of our male, sabotaging behavior was to increase Helen's and Marlene's doubts about themselves as leaders. For each of them, their lifelong conditioning that a woman ought to be a passive sweet thing came into play, and they gave up the helm because men "do it better."

If the reader thinks males are just threatened in the outdoors, look what happens to us indoors. First there is the machismo business, which is a cultural way of granting power to males. To the macho male, it is his role to take care of the woman, particularly in the face of imminent danger, and, in the course of things, he should never yield any power. In most organizational settings the male need to be in charge in the presence of females may be subtle, which may make it harder to identify than on a raft on a swift-flowing river. If all the male readers of this article would write down just one way to undermine the budding woman executive, there would be quite a list.

Judging from firsthand experience and others' reports, I believe that what happened on Raft No. 4, Inc. occurs in most organizations when women enter positions of leadership. An exception might be organizations that have been run by women from their inception. Because organizations are usually designed as pyramids, the moving-up process entails squeezing someone else out. The higher up the pyramid, the more the squeeze. As women enter the squeezing, men are doubly threatened; first, the number of pyramid squeeze players is increasing; second, because the new players are women, our masculinity is on the block. The resentment of men toward women managers is also exacerbated by the shrunken job market.

As more women become managers in organizations, there will have to be a shift in power. The men who hold that power in fierce competition with each other will not expand the competition by encouraging women to become part of the battle without considerable changes in their own consciousness. In a wilderness setting, all decisions, either one's own or the group's, have immediate consequences, such as being dumped out of the raft. The rightness or wrongness of decisions in organizations is not so obvious since a decision may have no perceptible effects for days or even months. It is during this time lag that the male unconscious activity can occur to undermine the female.

Will women in administrative positions be supported, ignored, or subconsciously sabotaged by men who find their power threatened? As most experienced administrators know, a major problem in running an organization is directly related to the level of subordinate support. How should the organization go? Straight ahead, hold, turn left, or turn right? These decisions are judgments that may be tough, but the leader must make them; and unless they are supported by the subordinates, they might as well never have been made.

A command of "hard right" can be executed as hard-hard, half-hard, and soft-hard, the last one being equal to just a facade of cooperation. That situation is the most dangerous one for the leader who presumes that orders are being executed, while in fact the raft is foundering. I suspect that one of the reasons that a woman has trouble is because the lack of support she receives from one man gets reinforced by others; it is a collective activity. Things might have been different on Raft No. 4 had we been willing to confront each other. It might have spoiled the fun, but we all might have learned something.

At first I thought there might not be much of an analogy between navigating a river and a big bureaucracy. Now I think there is. The requirements turn out to be different, and yet the same. The river is more easily understood: how it flows, its hydraulics, its sleepers, or its chutes, and women, like men, can learn these things. A big organization also has sleepers and chutes, but recognizing their existence is a far more political than intellectual task. Women trying to navigate most organizations may find them more complex than the Rogue, but they need to look for similar hazards. The sleepers and chutes will be vested groups of men, who, when their power is threatened, will pull any woman down for tinkering with their interests.

PART

II

Fitting In or Fighting Back

1
The Case of the Mismanaged Ms.

Sally Seymour

It started out as one of those rare quiet mornings when I could count on having the office to myself. The Mets had won the World Series the night before, and most of the people in the office had celebrated late into the night at a bar across the street. I'm a fan too, but they all like to go to one of those bars where the waitresses dress like slave girls and the few women customers have to run a mine field of leers when they go to a ladies' room labeled "Heifers." Instead, I watched the game at home with my husband and escaped a hangover.

So I was feeling pretty good, if a little smug, when Ruth Linsky, a sales manager here at Triton, stormed past my secretary and burst into my office. Before I could say good morning, she demanded to know what business it was of the company who she slept with and why. I didn't know what she was talking about, but I could tell it was serious. In fact, she was practically on the verge of tears, but I knew she wasn't the type to fly off the handle.

Ruth had been with the company for three years, and we all respected her as a sensible and intelligent woman. She had been top in her class at business school and we recruited her hard when she graduated, but she didn't join us for a couple of years. She's since proved to be one of our best people in sales, and I didn't want to lose her. She fumed around the room for a while, not making much sense, until I talked her into sitting down.

"I've had it with this place and the way it treats women!" she shouted.

I allowed her to let off some more steam for a minute or two, and then I tried to calm her down. "Look, Ruth," I said, "I can see you're upset, but I need to know exactly what's going on before I can help you."

"I'm not just upset, Barbara," she said, "I'm damned mad. I came over to Triton because I thought I'd get more chances to advance here, and I just found out that I was passed over for director of the marketing division and Dick Simon got it instead. You know that I've had three outstanding years at the company, and my performance reviews have been excellent. Besides, I was led to believe that I had a pretty good shot at the job."

"What do you mean, 'led to believe'?"

"Steve heard through the grapevine that they were looking for a new marketing director, and he suggested I put in my name," she said. "He knows my work from when we worked together over at Forge Techtronics, and he said he'd write a letter in support. I wouldn't have even known they were looking for someone if Steve hadn't tipped me off."

Steve Baines is vice president of manufacturing. He's certainly a respected senior person in the company and he pulls some weight, but he doesn't have sole control of the marketing position. The hierarchy doesn't work that way, and I tried to get Ruth to see that. "Okay, so Steve wrote a letter for you, but he's only one of five or six VPs who have input in executive hiring decisions. Of course it helps to have his support, but lots of other factors need to be considered as well."

"Come off it, Barbara," Ruth snapped. "You know as well as I do there's only one thing that really matters around here and that's whether you're one of the boys. I've got a meeting this afternoon with my lawyer, and I'm going to file a sexual discrimination suit, a sexual harassment suit, and whatever other kind of suit she can come up with. I've had it with this old-boy crap. The only reason I'm here is that, as human resources director, you should know what's going on around here."

So the stakes were even higher than I had thought; not only did it look like we might lose Ruth, but we also might have a lawsuit on our hands. And to top it off, with the discrimination issue Ruth might be trying to get back at us for promoting Dick. I felt strongly about the importance of this legal remedy, but I also knew that using it frivolously would only undermine women's credibility in legitimate cases.

"Ruth," I said, "I don't doubt your perceptions, but you're going to need some awfully strong evidence to back them up."

"You want evidence? Here's your evidence. Number one: 20% of the employees in this company are women. Not one is on the board of directors, and not one holds an executive-level position. You and I are the only two in mid-level positions. Number two: there's no way for women to move into the mid-level positions because they never know when they're available. When a vacancy comes up, the VPs—all men, of course—decide among themselves who should fill it. And then, over and over again I hear that some guy who hasn't worked half as hard as most of the women at his level has been given the plum. Number three: there are plenty of subtle and sometimes not-so-subtle messages around here that women are less than equal."

"Ruth, those are still pretty vague accusations," I interrupted. "You're going to have to come up with something more specific than feelings and suppositions."

"Don't worry, Barbara. Just keep listening and maybe you'll learn something about how this company you think so highly of operates. From the day Ed Coulter took over as vice president of marketing and became my boss, he's treated me differently from the male sales managers. Instead of saying good morning, he always has some comment about my looks—my dress is nice, or my hair looks pretty, or the color of my blouse brings out my eyes. I don't want to hear that stuff. Besides, he never comments on a guy's eyes. And then there's that calendar the sales reps have in their back office. Every time I go in there for a sales meeting, I feel like I've walked into a locker room."

So far, this all seemed pretty harmless to me, but I didn't want Ruth to feel I wasn't sympathetic. "To tell you the truth, Ruth, I'm not so sure all women here find compliments like that insulting, but maybe you can give me other examples of discriminatory treatment."

"You bet I can. It's not just in the office that these things happen. It's even worse in the field. Last month Ed and I and Bill, Tom, and Jack went out to Dryden Industries for a big project meeting. I'll admit I was a little nervous because there were some heavy hitters in the room, so I kept my mouth shut most of the morning. But I was a team member and I wanted to contribute.

"So when Ed stumbled at one point, I spoke up. Well, it was like I had committed a sacrilege in church. The Dryden guys just stared at me in surprise, and then they seemed actually angry. They ignored me completely. Later that afternoon, when I asked Ed why I had gotten that reaction, he chuckled a little and explained that since we hadn't been introduced by our specific titles, the Dryden guys had assumed I was a research assistant or a secretary. They thought I was being presumptuous. But when Ed explained who I was, they admitted that I had made an important point.

"But that wasn't all," she went on. "The next day, when we explained to them that I would be interviewing some of the factory foremen for a needs assessment, one of the executives requested that someone else do it because apparently there's a superstition about women on the factory floor bringing bad luck. Have you ever heard of anything so stupid? But that's not the worst of it. Ed actually went along with it. After I'd pulled his bacon out of the fire the day before. And when I nailed him for it, he had the gall to say 'Honey, whatever the client wants, the client gets.'

"Well, we got the contract, and that night we all went out to dinner and everything was hurray for our team. But then, when I figured we'd all go back to the hotel for a nightcap, Ed and the guys just kind of drifted off."

"Drifted off?" I asked.

"Yeah. To a bar. They wanted to watch some basketball game."

"And you weren't invited?"

"I wasn't invited and I wasn't disinvited," she said. "They acted like they didn't know what to say."

By this point Ruth had cooled down quite a bit, and although she still seemed angry, she was forthright in presenting her case. But now her manner changed. She became so agitated that she got up from her chair to stare out the window. After a few minutes, she sort of nodded her head, as if she had come to some private, difficult decision, and then crossed the room to sit down again. Looking at her lap and twisting a paper clip around in her hands, she spoke so softly that I had to lean forward to hear her.

"Barbara," she began, "what I'm going to tell you is, I hope, in confidence. It's not easy for me to talk about this because it's very personal and private, but I trust you and I want you to understand my position. So here goes. When Steve Baines and I were both at Forge, we had a brief affair. I was discreet about it; it never interfered with business, and we ended it shortly after we both came to work here. But we're still very close friends, and occasionally we have dinner or a drink together. But it's always as friends. I think Ed found out about it somehow. The day after I notified the head office that I wanted to be considered for the director position, Ed called me into his office and gave me a rambling lecture about how we have to behave like ladies and gentlemen these days because of lawsuits on sexual harassment.

"At the time, I assumed he was referring somehow to one of our junior sales reps who had gotten drunk at the Christmas party and made a fool of himself with a couple of secretaries; but later I began to think that the cryptic comment was meant for me. What's more, I think Ed used that rumor about my relationship with Steve to block my promotion. And that, Barbara, is pure, sexist, double-standard hypocrisy because I can name you at least five guys at various levels in this company who have had affairs with colleagues and clients, and Ed is at the top of the list."

I couldn't deny the truth of Ruth's last statement, but that wasn't the point, or not yet. First I had to find out which, if any, of her accusations were true. I told her I needed some time and asked if she could give me a week before calling in a lawyer. She said no way. Having taken the first step, she was anxious to take the next, especially since she didn't believe things would change at Triton anyway. We dickered back and forth, but all I could get from her was a promise to hold off for 24 hours. Not much of a concession, but it was better than nothing.

Needless to say, I had a lot to think about and not very much time to do it in. It was curious that this complaint should come shortly after our organization had taken steps to comply with affirmative action policies by issuing a companywide memo stating that we would continue to recruit, employ, train, and promote individuals without regard to race, color, religion, sex, age, national origin, physical or mental handicap, or status as a disabled veteran or veteran of the Vietnam era. And we did this to prevent any problems in the future, not because we'd had trouble in the past. In fact, in my five years as HRM director, I'd never had a sexual discrimination or harassment complaint.

But now I was beginning to wonder whether there had never been grounds for complaint or whether the women here felt it was useless or even dangerous to complain. If it was the latter, how had I contributed to allowing that feeling to exist? And this thought led me to an even more uncomfortable one: Had I been co-opted into ignoring injustices in a system that, after all, did pretty well by me? Was I afraid to slap the hand that buttered my bread?

Questioning one's own motives may be enlightening, but it's also time consuming, and I had more pressing matters to deal with before I could indulge in what would likely be a painful self-analysis. I asked my secretary to find George Drake, CEO of Triton, and get him on the phone. In the meantime, I wrote down as much as I could remember of what Ruth had just told me. When George finally called, I told him I knew his schedule was full but we had an emergency of sorts on our hands and I needed an hour of his time this morning. I also asked that Ed Coulter be called into the meeting. George told me I had the hour.

When I got to George's office, Ed and George were already waiting. They were undoubtedly curious about why I had called this meeting, but as I've seen people do in similar situations, they covered their anxiety with chitchat about ball games and hangovers. I was too impatient for these rituals, so I cut the conversation short and told them that we were going to have a serious lawsuit on our hands in a matter of days if we didn't act very quickly. That got their attention, so I proceeded to tell Ruth's story. When I began, George and Ed seemed more surprised than anything else, but as I built up Ruth's case their surprise turned to concern. When I finished, we all sat in silence for I don't know how long and then George asked Ed for comments.

"Well, George," Ed said, "I don't know what to say. Ruth certainly was a strong contender for the position, and her qualifications nearly equaled Dick's, but it finally came down to the fact that Dick had the seniority and a little more experience in the industrial sector. When you've got two almost equally qualified candidates, you've got to distinguish them somehow. The decision came down to the wire, which in this case was six months seniority and a few more visits to factory sites."

"Were those the only criteria that made a difference in the decision?" George wanted to know.

"Well, not exactly. You know as well as I do that we base hiring decisions on a lot of things. On one hand, we look at what's on paper: years at the company, education, experience, recommendations. But we also rely on intuition, our feel for the situation. Sometimes, you don't know exactly why, but you just feel better about some people than others, and I've learned that those gut reactions are pretty reliable. The other VPs and I all felt good about Dick. There's something about him—he's got the feel of a winner. You know? He's confident—not arrogant—but solid and really sharp. Bruce had him out to the club a couple of times, and I played squash with him all last winter. We got to know him and we liked what we saw; he's a family man, kids in school here, could use the extra money, and is looking to stick around for a while. None of these things mean a lot by themselves, of course, but together they add up."

"Don't get me wrong. I like Ruth too. She's very ambitious and one of our best. On the other hand, I can't say that I or any of the VPs know her as well as we know Dick. Of course, that's not exactly Ruth's fault, but there it is."

I had to be careful with the question I wanted Ed to respond to next because Ruth had asked for my confidence about the affair. I worded it this way: "Ed, did any part of your decision take into account Ruth's relationship with anyone else at the company?"

The question visibly disturbed Ed. He walked across the room and bummed a cigarette from me—he had quit last week—before answering: "Okay, I didn't want to go into this, but since you brought it up. . . . There's a rumor—well it's stronger than a rumor—that Ruth is more than professionally involved with Steve Baines—I mean she's having an, ah, sexual affair with him. Now before you tell me that's none of my business, let me tell you about some homework I did on this stuff. Of course it's real tricky. It turns out there are at least two court cases that found sexual discrimination where an employer involved in a sexual relationship with an employee promoted that person over more qualified candidates.

"So here's what that leaves us with: we've got Steve pushing his girlfriend for the job. You saw the letter he wrote. And we've got Dick with seniority. So if we go with Ruth, what's to keep Dick from charging Steve and the company on two counts of sexual discrimination: sexual favoritism because Ruth is Steve's honey and reverse discrimination because we pass over a better qualified man just to get a woman into an executive position. So we're damned if we do and damned if we don't. We've got lawsuits if we don't advance Dick, and, so you tell me, lawsuits if we don't advance Ruth!"

We let that sink in for a few seconds. Then George spoke up: "What evidence do you have, Ed, that Steve and Ruth are having an affair?" he asked.

"Look, I didn't hire some guy to follow them around with a camera, if that's what you mean," Ed said. "But come on, I wasn't born yesterday; you can't keep that kind of hanky-panky a secret forever. Look at the way she dresses; she obviously enjoys men looking at her, especially Steve. In fact, I saw them having drinks together at Dino's the other night and believe me, they didn't look like they were talking business. All that on top of the rumors, you put two and two together."

Well, that did it for me. I'd been trying to play the objective observer and let Ed and George do all the talking, but Ed's last comment, along with some budding guilt about my own blindness to certain things at Triton that Ruth had pointed out, drove me out in the open. "Come off it, Ed," I said. "That's not evidence, that's gossip."

Now Ed turned on me: "Look," he shouted, "I didn't want to talk about this, but now that you've brought it up, I'll tell you something else. Even if we didn't have to worry about this sexual discrimination business, I still wouldn't back Ruth for the director's job." He calmed down a bit. "No offense, Barbara, but I just don't think women work out as well as men in certain positions. Human resources is one thing. It's real soft, person-to-person stuff. But factories are still a man's world. And I'm not talking about what I want it to be like. I'm talking facts of life.

"You see what happens when we send a woman out on some jobs, especially in the factories. To be any good in marketing you have to know how to relate to your client; that means getting to know him, going out drinking with him, talking sports, hunting, whatever he's interested in. A lot of our clients feel uncomfortable around a woman in business. They know how to relate to their wives, mothers, and girlfriends, but when a woman comes to the office and wants to talk a deal on industrial drills—well, they don't know what to do.

"And then there's the plain fact that you can't depend on a woman the way you can on a guy. She'll get married and her husband will get transferred, or she'll have a baby and want time off and not be able to go on the road as much. I know, Barbara, you probably think I'm a pig, or whatever women's libbers call guys like me these days. But from where I'm sitting, it just made good business sense to choose Dick over Ruth."

"Ed, I don't believe it," I said. "The next thing you'll tell me is that women ought to stay at home, barefoot and pregnant." There was a long silence after that—my guess was that I had hit on exactly what Ed thought. At least he didn't deny it. Ed stared at the rug, and George frowned at his coffee cup. I tried to steer the conversation back to the subject at hand, but it dwindled into another silence. George took a few notes and then told Ed he could go back to work. I assumed I was excused too, but as I started to leave, George called me back.

"Barbara, I'm going to need your help thinking through this mess," he said. "Of course we've got to figure out how we can avoid a lawsuit before the day is out, but I also want to talk about what we can do to avoid more lawsuits in the future. While Ed was talking I took some notes, and I've got maybe four or five points I think we ought to hash out. I'm not saying we're going to come up with all the answers today, but it'll be a start. You ready?"

"Shoot."

"Okay, let's do the big one first," he began. "What should I have done or not done to avoid this situation? I mean, I was just patting myself on the back for being so proactive when I sent out that memo letting everyone know the company policy on discrimination. I wrote it not thinking we had any problem at Triton. But just in case we did, I figured that memo would take care of it."

"Well, it looks like it's not enough just to have a corporate policy if the people in the ranks aren't on board. Obviously it didn't have much of an effect on Ed."

"So what am I supposed to do? Fire Ed?"

Being asked for my honest opinion by my CEO was a new experience for me and I appreciated it, but I wasn't going to touch that last question with a ten-foot pole. Instead I went on to another aspect: "And even if you get your managers behind you, your policy won't work if the people it's supposed to help don't buy it. Ruth was the first woman to complain around here. Are the others afraid to speak up? Or do they feel like Ed about a woman's place, or have husbands who do? Maybe they lack confidence even to try for better jobs, that is, if they knew about them."

"Okay," he said, "I'll admit that our system of having the VPs make recommendations, our 'old-boy network,' as Ruth called it, does seem to end up excluding women, even though the exclusion isn't intentional. And it's not obvious discrimination, like Ed's claim that Ruth is unqualified for a position because she is a woman. But wouldn't open job posting take away our right to manage as we see fit? Maybe we should concentrate instead on getting more women into the social network, make it an old boys' and old girls' club?"

"To tell you the truth, George, I don't much want to play squash with you," I replied, "but maybe we're getting off the subject. The immediate question seems to be how we're going to get more women into executive positions here, or, more specifically, do we give Ruth the director of marketing position that we just gave Dick?"

"On that score, at least, it seems to me that Ed has a strong argument," George said. "Dick is more qualified. You can't get around that."

I had wanted to challenge Ed on this point when he brought it up earlier, but I wasn't quite sure of myself then. Now that George was asking me for advice and seemed to be taking what I had to say seriously, I began to think that I might have something valuable to offer. So I charged right in. "George, maybe we're cutting too fine a line with this qualifications business. I know a lot of people think affirmative action means promoting the unqualified over the qualified to achieve balance. I think that argument is hogwash at best and a wily diversion tactic at worst. To my mind, Ruth and Dick are equally qualified, or equal enough. And wouldn't it make good business sense to get a diverse set of perspectives—women's, men's, blacks', whites'— in our executive group?"

"But isn't that reverse discrimination—not promoting Dick because he's a man? How would a judge respond to that? That's a question for a lawyer."

George leaned forward. "Let's talk about my last point, the one I think we've both been avoiding. What about this affair between Ruth and Steve? Boy, this is one reason why women in the work force are such trouble—no, just joking, Barbara, sorry about that. Look, I don't like lawsuits any more than anyone else, but I'd do anything to avoid this one. We'd be a laughing stock if it got out that Triton promoted unqualified people because they slept with the boss. I don't know how I'd explain that one to my wife."

"Look, George," I said, "in the first place, Dick's superior qualifications are debatable; in the second place, we have no proof that Ruth and Steve are involved in that way; and in the third place, what if they were once involved but no longer are? Does a past relationship condemn them for life? Isn't there a statute of limitations on that kind of thing, or are we going to make her put a scarlet letter on her briefcase? I thought these discrimination laws were supposed to protect women, but now it looks like a woman can be denied a promotion because someone thinks she's a floozy."

"Wait a second, Barbara. Don't make me look like such a prig," George said. "I realize that when men and women work together sexual issues are bound to crop up. I just don't know what I'm supposed to do about it, if anything. In some cases a woman may welcome a guy coming on to her, but what if it's her boss? And then there's that subtle stuff Ruth brought up—the calendar, dirty jokes, the male employees excluding women by going to bars to watch TV—and other women. And Ruth's treatment at that factory—how can we control our clients? I'm not sure these are things you can set policy on, but I am sure that I can't ignore them any longer."

And there we were. All the issues were on the table, and we had about 21 hours to make our decisions and act on them.

What Would You Do?

DONALD J. COMEAU

The facts indicate clear discriminatory practices.

It is clear that Triton's historical methods of hiring, developing, and ultimately promoting its people systematically discriminate against women. The mere issuance of a "policy statement" from the CEO without the proper training and understanding of the people who must carry out the policy is ludicrous. Triton has obviously made an attempt to bring in qualified, high-potential women but has paid no attention to integrating them into the old-boy network, and even less attention to evaluating their qualifications on a nondiscriminatory basis.

It's not unusual that these issues came to light as a result of a specific situation. As Triton brings more highly educated and trained women into the company, management must change its policies on development and promotion.

The facts as presented indicate clear discriminatory practices. Since a possible lawsuit is a real threat, Barbara and George's time should be spent deciding: how they will handle the decision to promote Dick ahead of Ruth, what steps must be taken to correct the practices that put them into this situation, and how to handle Ruth.

The decision to promote Dick must stand. To do otherwise would put Triton at risk of losing two very good people—Dick and Ruth. Reversing the decision, while it would make Ruth director of the marketing division, would also position her for failure. The organization would perceive the reversal to have occurred simply because she was a woman, not because of her qualifications and ability to do the job. Dick, on the other hand, might resign and/or file his own lawsuit.

George as CEO must institute an affirmative action plan that his office controls and follows up. It must be understood and practiced at all levels of the organization and be recognized as part of the company's business plan, on which managers are evaluated. Important elements in the plan must include but not be limited to:

Elimination of the old-boy network.

A promotion policy based on qualifications—perhaps a bid system or other nondiscriminatory method of judging abilities.

A comprehensive development program for all managers to immediately begin educating them in Triton's affirmative action plan, with ongoing followup sessions.

Individual counseling that addresses women in management and how to deal with the issues, for example, for people like Ed. In this case, an affair should only be a consideration when job performance is affected, and that applies equally to men and women.

Communication of the plan to all employees and clients.

Once the outline of this plan is put on paper, George and Barbara should sit with Ruth and talk with her about the following:

The decision on Dick and the reasons for going ahead with him as the new director of the marketing division.

Plans for revitalizing an affirmative action strategy.

Since Ruth obviously has some strong and constructive feelings about integrating women into Triton, offer her the opportunity to work directly with Barbara and George to develop and implement the revitalized affirmative action plan.

If after this discussion Ruth decides to file a lawsuit, then she should do so; the affirmative action plan, however, must be carried out.

ZOE COULSON

It takes more than a memo to promote qualified women.

Women—and men—climbing career ladders need to recognize that so-called old-fashioned values, ethics, and morals still have credence. Many men and women heading today's major American companies and participating on boards of directors have been molded by another era; it is not surprising that they use their own standards when evaluating the personal traits of someone being considered for advancement.

In this case, Ruth's corporate accomplishments are not reported as exceptional to the man's; in fact, Dick "had seniority and a little more experience in the industrial sector," according to Ed, a vice president. Ed's subjective evaluations, however, seemed to be influenced by traditional views some men have about women; a woman working in industry may be unsettling to a man raised in a background where women only worked at home.

Since men like Ed make management decisions, it is essential for women with high corporate goals to recognize the corporation's customs as well as management's standards on personal characteristics, and act accordingly. After the successful team project, Ruth did not mention if each male specifically was invited to celebrate afterwards; it sounds as if a spontaneous team event happened and Ruth didn't "read" it. While some men also don't correctly evaluate such customs, women, who may be new to these environments, need to be especially aware.

Different corporations have different customs, and if a company's atmosphere is tightly traditional, people of high ambition should respond accordingly. In this case, when Ruth was employed in another company, she did not consider the implications of her personal actions (her affair with Steve) if she changed companies. But the custom of informal meetings between candidates and other officers was one of Ed's methods of evaluating promotability, and Ruth's "reputation" didn't encourage the informal interview custom. In today's world of corporate mergers and executive job changing, managers overlap between companies and, indeed, areas of the country, so implications can be far-reaching.

While the people in this case are in middle management, they should be aware that traditional values and customs are important to upper management in many of today's big companies. And top executives send down signals; how they act is how they expect their peers to act. They may not promote someone with entirely different customs from theirs.

Ruth commented that at the previous company her brief affair with Steve "was discreet; it never interfered with business, and we ended it." Her previous personal behavior introduced an issue.

This case does not state the marital status of these employees. As the legal counsel of a big corporation commented recently, "When a senior manager 'bends the rules' on one corporate policy, he sends a message that his employees apply to lots of rules," which can lead to staff dishonesty. Marriage, of course, is a legal contract, as well as a personal commitment; therefore, some corporate managers use fidelity as one criteria when promoting someone.

In another corporation, the chief executive officer was removed by his board of directors a few years ago because of an extramarital affair. In another company, an officer was asked to resign because of his approach to a secretary. In yet another, the president suggested to a divorced senior executive that he marry the woman with whom he was living; the board chairman was a traditionalist. The man married the woman and probably removed a concern of the board.

Since these situations have affected men's careers, women need to be doubly cautious. Meeting with a male business friend occasionally for a drink or dinner should cause no stir in today's world if the ambiance of the place is pleasant and if the couple's demeanor portrays friendship, not sex; many corporate cultures accept this. In other environments, however, even a meeting with a nonemployee date that might reveal sexual overtones should take place in private, or at least not in a public place where a "message" might be extended.

Since Ruth seems to be one of few women in her company, she is more visible than a man, whether she likes it or not. She needs to recognize that she is being reviewed at all times.

All this is not to say there is no problem. Even though George sent a policy statement to staff on affirmative action, women in this corporation are still at risk. It takes more than a memo to promote qualified women! Senior management could consider these and perhaps other steps to send strong signals to employees:

Should men be trained in reviewing women's qualifications?

Should there be special programs for all minorities on "keys to success"?

Can top officers become informal mentors to potential executive women—and men—so that they better understand the company's customs?

Should male managers be evaluated on their progress in promoting women?

Since Ruth has stated her dissatisfaction, in my opinion she has two courses of action. She could continue to execute her job as well as possible and avoid situations that might be misinterpreted by associates. Or she could go work for another company and learn its pattern at the beginning.

With more dedicated, educated women in the work force, some discriminatory beliefs about women's roles indeed will erode in the future. Women like Ruth, however, should learn now how to put themselves in the man's chair, to better understand and respect male values. Also, women who are achievers are setting examples for women who follow them, so they have another responsibility.

Top executives can make efforts to discuss their values (and practice them), so aspiring men and women managers can learn their scoring system.

It is to be hoped that Ruth will now understand the scorecard at her company better so that next time an opening occurs she will be judged with higher points.

R. MARILYN LEE

All employees should feel comfortable and have an equal chance to advance.

Triton is about to have its first sex discrimination and sexual harassment complaint. This case has it all—a predominantly male work force with an old-boy environment, a secretive promotion system, a qualified woman loses a job to a qualified man, rumors of a personal relationship, sexual stereotypes, and good old-fashioned bias.

How did a nice company like Triton with a concerned CEO like George end up in a mess like this? From the facts given, it appears that Triton hasn't done well in keeping pace with a changing workplace. Women generally make up more than 45% of the nation's employees, yet Triton has only 20%, low for even an industrial setting. There are no women in the executive group at Triton and only two in middle management. From Ruth's perspective, the women at Triton are made uncomfortable by the good-old-boy atmosphere of talking sports and going to bars. Management has an antidiscrimination policy but apparently has taken no steps to make the work environment hospitable for all employees.

The case does not look good for Triton. Ed found Dick's and Ruth's qualifications to be nearly identical. The additional criteria that Ed considered—intuition, socializing with Dick at club events, Dick's being a family man who needed the extra money—were subjective at best and irrelevant at worst. Add Ed's belief that women don't belong in certain work settings, his discriminatory treatment of Ruth, and his hasty assumptions about Ruth's relationship with Steve, and this case could be a plaintiff lawyer's dream come true.

Can the problem be resolved in the next 24 hours? Probably not, but there is time for Barbara to review the facts and discuss options with George and Ed. Triton's legal department or outside lawyers should be consulted as management proceeds.

Here is one approach the company might take. Barbara could meet with Ruth the next day and explain that the company takes seriously her claims of discrimination. Let Ruth know that George has been briefed and has asked Barbara to immediately proceed with an investigation that will include more detailed interviews with Ruth, Ed, and others.

It would also be a good idea to find out what Ruth wants at this point. When she first saw Barbara, she was very upset. Barbara needs to find out if Ruth really would like to continue working for Triton, or have recent events soured that possibility? If the situation is salvageable, Barbara should ask Ruth to give the company time to do the right thing. (That does not mean giving her the disputed promotion. Since it appears that the company's selection of Dick has been announced, it would be unwise to reverse the decision and thereby create a second personnel dispute.)

Either Ruth will agree to work with the human resources manager on the complaint, or she will tell her that it has gone too far and she would rather go to court. Perhaps the prospect of a future promotion for Ruth can be suggested and discussed with George. In either event, the company should investigate her claim, take appropriate corrective action, and move forward with new personnel programs.

The long-term goal for Triton's management should be to open up the atmosphere so that all employees are comfortable and have an equal chance to advance. Some steps are quite simple.

First, an internal job posting procedure should be established. Promotional openings should not be communicated only through the grapevine. Job posting increases accountability in hiring decisions and encourages women and minorities to apply.

Second, supervisory training on equal opportunity and a diversified work force is clearly needed. Managers and supervisors should understand that offensive language and insensitive actions can create a hostile, discriminatory environment. Ruth's case contains several examples: calling her "honey," not introducing her on sales calls, not including her in social activities on business trips, and allowing locker-room calendars to be posted on office walls. Many men are genuinely surprised that some of these actions are offensive. A discussion between male and female colleagues, including suggested ways to handle travel assignments and introduce new employees, would help.

In addition, training can address sexual stereotyping. For instance, Ed assumes that a saleswoman would not relate well to a client in a factory setting because she may not talk about hunting or sports. Ruth has already shown that notion to be false because she is one of Triton's best salespeople. Ed also wrongly assumes that women leave jobs at a greater rate than men. Men tend to leave jobs just as often—for promotional opportunities, career changes, and, yes, even because their wives have been transferred to new jobs.

A good training program will also develop ways to deal with customers who seem to prefer a male account executive. Here Ed might have suggested to Dryden Industries that Ruth was one of Triton's top people and capable of doing the needs assessment, or that Ruth work with a man to do the survey more quickly.

Training can instill a better understanding of affirmative action and employment law generally. Ed, playing armchair lawyer, is confused about reverse discrimination. Selecting a qualified woman candidate over a qualified man is lawful when women are underrepresented in that job category—certainly the case at Triton.

Training classes could review Triton's employment data and identify the problem areas. Affirmative action hires and special attention to the promotion of women and minorities may be needed until the work force is more balanced. Once employees understand that concept, some of the anxiety about affirmative action is eased.

Ed will need some individual coaching since he obviously has strong opinions on this subject and may adversely influence others he supervises.

Third, Triton's management must show that its affirmative action policies have a clear direction. Issuing an antidiscrimination policy is fine but is a small piece of a larger pie. The company needs to take firm steps to increase the number of women in the general work force and in management.

A directive from the top is always the best way to start. George should meet with his vice presidents and convey his expectations: that they will increase the number of women employees in each department where women are underrepresented and establish programs to assure career development for women. George could make affirmative action goals a part of each executive's annual bonus plan and withhold payment if goals are not met. It is not surprising to find that those people who are good at meeting sales and other business goals become equally good at meeting affirmative action goals, once the company's commitment is made clear.

Last, the human resources department should become more involved with the promotion process. If Triton had well-defined affirmative action goals, Barbara could have advised Ed that all things being equal, Ruth should have been selected over Dick in order to diversify the director group. Promotional selection by a committee of vice presidents appears to be a holdover from the old days and does cloud the issue of who is actually making the promotional decision. Hence, Ruth's past affair with Steve is brought up even though Ruth, in marketing, does not have a direct reporting relationship to Steve, in production.

As Triton implements some of these long-range solutions, there will be plenty of questions and issues to address along the way. Barbara is perceptive to acknowledge that other women may also have complaints but may have been afraid to come forward. The issues are clearly under the surface, and it would be far better to take remedial action now before another "case of the mismanaged Ms." appears.

JOSEPH POSNER

Coulter has to go.

Ed Coulter is going to cost this company some real money. Any way you look at it, the company is going to have to pay some big bucks to get out of the mess in which it finds itself and, perhaps more important, to prevent the same thing from happening in the future.

Apparently, Triton already gave Dick Simon the promotion to director of the marketing division. Even without considering the issue of reverse discrimination, the company can't very well take the promotion away from him. If it tried to do this, Dick would probably have a good lawsuit against the company without regard to whether the action constituted reverse discrimination. At least under California law, I think that he could sue and win.

When Ruth came into Barbara's office, she had more suspicions than facts. But her suspicions proved to be far more true than even Ruth probably realized. It is apparent to me that this company, which seems to be a fairly good-sized operation, has engaged in a systematic pattern of making it virtually impossible for a woman to receive any significant promotion. On the one hand, you had Ruth with an outstanding record, a sensible, intelligent person, and quite stable; the fact that she was provoked by this incident is not only understandable because of its gravity but it also shows the extreme impact on her.

Taken by itself, deciding to promote Dick or to promote Ruth to the director's job could probably each be defended, as they appear evenly matched. But when I see: (1) all the top jobs controlled by a tight group in the old-boy network and the openings not made known to others; (2) the situation at the customer's factory where Ed refused to back up Ruth by telling the customer that Ruth was the person in charge and had to do the interviewing; (3) the use of a mere suspicion about a subject which is none of Ed's business in the first place, i.e., Ruth's friendship with Steve; (4) Ed's admission that a factor in promotions is off-hours socializing at the country club (leading to the conclusion that off-hours socializing at the local bar is a part of business activities); (5) Ed's candid statement that he doesn't think women are good for certain jobs because they should stick to things that are in his words "real soft, person to person"; (6) his statement that women aren't dependable because of marriage, dependence on a husband, pregnancy, or the like—these factors all add up to the reality that the company did exactly what Ruth suspected it of doing.

In that connection, the other points, such as the fact that there is a pinup calendar in the sales room, don't carry a lot of weight with me. In a trial, these, however, as well as the most important factors I already mentioned, would certainly be something for the jury to think about.

In my opinion, Ed Coulter has to go. The company simply cannot afford to keep a man in his position with his attitudes and demonstrated actions. Perhaps a transfer could be arranged for him and/or a job found for him at another company or related entity. But one thing is for sure—the longer he is there, the more he is going to cost the company, if not today, then later.

Next, even George, the president, needs to have his consciousness raised. He is not in the same league with Ed, by any means, but he needs to realize that he has a problem, and he needs to do something about it. That would include calling together the five or six remaining vice presidents and laying the law down in no uncertain terms that the way people are selected for the top jobs is going to change, and change now. And then George has to monitor the situation to see that his subordinates do what he tells them.

This leaves us with the big question, what to do about Ruth, and this is a real dilemma. If Ruth were to sue, and if she ever could get testimony about the conversation in George's office, she would win in a walk. And since the company appears to have been selecting people for the top jobs this way for some time, I am willing to bet that there are more "Ruths" out there.

The company should think about a substantial monetary settlement with Ruth *right now*, whether she stays with Triton or not. Certainly, nothing should be said to her about leaving, and she should be promised that she would be the preferred candidate for the next slot that opens up. Moreover, Triton should look around to see if there are any such positions to which she could be promoted now. In addition, the company should think about doing some reorganization, if that is possible and makes good business sense. The one thing that Ruth will have to accept is the fact that Triton can't very well take back its promotion of Dick Simon.

T. GARY ROGERS

Put the responsibility for human resources where it belongs.

If George Drake were to ask me for advice on dealing with the issues raised by the Ruth Linsky controversy at Triton, I would offer him the following five observations:

1. Triton's policy is equal opportunity, and Ruth hasn't had it yet. Affirmative action has to be more than a toothless memo. Equal opportunity in hiring means the person with the best *relevant* qualifications (more on that below) gets the job. Triton has an obligation to let its people know when an opening occurs and to interview any applicants from within the company who may be qualified. Because minorities and women *are* often discriminated against in hiring decisions, Triton must be especially careful to ensure such candidates for promotion a fair opportunity to present their credentials and make their case. Ruth clearly deserved an interview for this job, but she did not really get one, and this must be remedied immediately.

2. The relevant qualifications are only those related to job effectiveness. Triton's first responsibility is to its shareholders. Its managers should be selected on the basis of their ability to further the company's goals and maximize its earnings. In choosing between Ruth Linsky and Dick Simon for director of the marketing division, only factors that affect job performance in that role should pertain. Ruth's relationship with Steve Baines is irrelevant unless it somehow affects her ability to perform the job. The assertion that she will get married and move or want time off to have a family is not germane unless those really are her plans. Similarly, Dick's being a family man, or needing a raise, or playing squash obviously should not enter into the equation.

On the other hand, it *is* appropriate to consider that a director of marketing in the industrial drill business has to deal and be effective with many types of men, including some who have deep-seated (albeit unfair) prejudices toward women in business. Triton has no obligation to change the culture of its industry and has to be realistic about the skills and attitudes its managers require to cope effectively within that culture. Therefore, it *is* appropriate to compare Ruth and Dick in terms of their maturity, experience, and demonstrated ability to function in what is largely a "man's world," even though that requirement poses a much tougher challenge for Ruth than it does for Dick.

3. Let Ed Coulter make the decision, but require him to explain his thinking. Ed is charged with responsibility for marketing at Triton and has the right and duty to select the management team for his department. If Ed wants the advice of the other vice presidents, that's fine, but the final decision should be his responsibility alone—not that of a committee. In making his decision, however, Ed must comply with the company's affirmative action program and be able to satisfy his boss that he has done so.

Given the sensitivity of this matter and the questions about Ed's understanding of the issues, George should have a long talk with Ed about equal opportunity, relevant hiring criteria, and the law. At the end of this discussion, George should ask Ed to interview Ruth with an open mind, reconsider his decision, and then come back and share his thinking with George. In his conversation with Ed, George should be careful to have Ed understand that he is not campaigning for Ruth but only ensuring that she receive fair consideration as an applicant for the job.

4. Don't let potential lawsuits affect your business decisions. The real issue for George is whether Triton's policies and practices comply with his desires (and the law) on an ongoing basis. If they do, George should assume Triton will prevail, if sued. Unfortunately, defending lawsuits, particularly in the personnel arena, has become a cost of doing business, even for the best-managed companies. If George is satisfied that Triton is acting appropriately, then he should not let Ruth's threat of legal action affect his thinking—except, perhaps, as an indication of immaturity or poor judgment on her part.

5. Consider reassigning human resources responsibilities at Triton. The first and most important responsibility of any manager is for his (or her) human resources, and good managers will demand direct control over the hiring, training, motivating, and developing of their people. Triton appears to exhibit a problem common to many companies with a high-profile human resources department—management

has abrogated much of its most important responsibility. Triton's managers should understand, be thinking about, and be experienced with the subtleties of equal opportunity and other people-related issues. At Triton, it appears the human resources department "takes care of that."

For example, it would have been much more appropriate and efficient for Ruth to take her complaint directly to Ed—or to George, if necessary—rather than to the human resources department. Choosing properly between Ruth Linsky and Dick Simon requires integrating judgments about job requirements, industry culture, and individual capabilities. If Ed Coulter is qualified for his job, he should be able to make these judgments appropriately without help from a staff department. If Ed cannot be trusted to do this, he should be replaced. George should reduce the role of his corporate staff in personnel matters to only technical support and record keeping and put the responsibility for human resources where it belongs—squarely in the hands of his managers.

Note

At the time of this article's publication Donald J. Conneau was corporate senior vice president of the Stop & Shop Companies, Inc. Zoe Coulson was vice president of consumer issues for the Campbell Soup Company. R. Marilyn Lenn was corporate director of human resources for *The Times Mirror Company.* Joseph Posner was a trial and appellate lawyer in the Los Angeles area. T. Gary Rogers was chairman of the board and chief executive officer of Dreyer's Grand Ice Cream, Inc.

2
The Case of the Hidden Harassment

Daniel Niven

Jerry Tarkwell, a real estate lending manager at Filmore Trust, marched out of his office toward the associate's wing of the bank's eighteenth-floor offices. "I need the Thompson Properties file right away," Tarkwell said to the associates' secretary. "Do you know where I can find it?"

"It's probably on Jill's computer table. I was helping her enter the new figures this morning."

"Thanks." Tarkwell headed down the hallway and knocked on the door marked "Jill McNair, Associate." McNair didn't answer, so he opened the door and walked over to the computer table piled high with folders. As he shuffled through the files, Tarkwell glanced at what was written on the computer screen. It was an electronic mail message McNair had sent earlier.

Can you walk me out again tonight? He's in today and I'm sure he'll be waiting for me. He leaned up against me when I was at the coffee machine this morning and whispered some disgusting stuff about how great he is in bed. I don't want another episode like the one in the hallway Monday night. I should have left when you did, but I thought he'd already gone.

I'm sorry you have to put up with this. Get back to me. I'll be ready to go whenever you are.

"Oh, that's awful." Tarkwell felt sickened as he got up to leave. "God, I wonder who's doing this?" He grabbed the Thompson Properties file, returned to his own office, and called the company's equal employment officer.

"Tarkwell was in your office a little while ago looking for the

Thompson file," shouted the secretary as Jill McNair walked briskly down the hall.

"Damn, I was supposed to hand that over to him an hour ago," McNair thought as she opened her door. The computer screen immediately caught her eye. "Oh no," she gasped, "I can't believe I left that on." The ring of her phone made her jump.

"Hi, Jill, it's Jerry. I'd like to talk to you right away. Can you come down to my office?"

"Sure," she said weakly and then hung up the phone. "I'll bet he read it," she thought. "What am I going to do now?"

McNair knocked on Tarkwell's door and went in. "Sit down, Jill. I have something rather disturbing to discuss with you," Tarkwell began. "I went into your office to pick up the Thompson file. I'm afraid I read what was on your computer screen."

Jill looked at him angrily. She clenched her fists in her lap.

"Let me tell you first how sorry I am that you've been . . . put in that kind of situation." Tarkwell shifted uncomfortably. He was having trouble finding words that wouldn't embarrass them both. "I need to know who's been doing this to you so we can put a stop to it. I called the equal employment officer, and she explained the steps to resolving a case of this sort. First you . . ."

McNair cut him off. "You had no right to read my personal e-mail, and you had no right to call EEO before talking to me. This is my problem not yours, and I don't want this getting around. Do you have any idea what can happen to me and to my career if people find out about this?"

"I didn't tell them who'd be bringing the complaint," Tarkwell said. "You just have to write a letter, and they do an investigation."

"Don't you understand?" she asked, seething. "It would be his word against mine, and he's senior to me." She wished she hadn't let that slip. "I'm the one who's going to get hurt. If this gets investigated by EEO, everyone in this building could be questioned. I'll probably get transferred, and then I won't have a chance at promotion. And who'd want to work with me? Every man in the company would be afraid I'd report him if he so much as opened a door for me."

"Look," Tarkwell reasoned, "nobody here has to find out. I'm sure the EEO will do whatever you feel is best. You know you can't go on working under these conditions."

"I won't have my privacy invaded," McNair said flatly. "There's nothing you can do."

"But it's a federal law," Tarkwell demanded. "This company has to maintain a workplace free of sexual coercion, and as your manager, I have to report this. It's company policy."

"I've got too much at stake here," McNair answered, reaching for the door. "So just stay out of it, Jerry. I can take care of it myself."

How Can Tarkwell Best Resolve This Issue?

Five experts on sexual harassment in the workplace examine his options.

CHERYL WANG

Jerry, although I know you will be talking to lawyers, people from human resources, and equal employment officers about Jill McNair's case, perhaps I can offer you another perspective—the perspective of someone who understands what Jill is going through. I too was a victim of sexual harassment.

In my case, however, the managers were not as enlightened as you are. They heard my harasser make comments like "let's go see a porno film" or "let me pet your sweater." They knew that intelligent women like me weren't getting assigned to exciting, high-visibility projects. They saw that women were leaving the department, one by one. And they did nothing. You, on the other hand, have recognized that what Jill is experiencing is sexual harassment. And, most important, you are treating this as a serious problem.

Unlike the managers I encountered, you want to help. But you won't be helping Jill by forcing her to bring a complaint against the harasser. She is already a victim of someone else's unwanted actions. Don't compound her sense of victimization by pushing her into another situation she doesn't want to be in.

Perhaps the best way to help Jill is to show her how to take control. Show her that there *are* options. But first make damn sure that those options really do exist.

Find out what the sexual harassment policy in your office is. Does the message that sexual harassment is illegal and will not be tolerated come through loud and clear? Does that message come from top management? Are seminars held so that all employees understand what sexual harassment is and what to do if they encounter it? Is there a complaint system in place? If so, does it work? Do the employees trust it?

I suspect that the answer to these questions is no. If Filmore Trust did have an effective way of dealing with sexual harassment, Jill wouldn't feel as if she had to accept harassment as a necessary evil of her job. And managers like you would know specific steps to take that wouldn't jeopardize the victim or the company.

If you really want to help Jill and Filmore Trust, you must convince the company to educate its employees and to establish a good system for handling sexual harassment complaints. Ultimately, you will be helping not only Jill but other potential victims as well. The chances are good that Jill is not the only person at Filmore Trust experiencing sexual harassment.

These are long-term solutions that will take time to implement; however, you and Jill also need immediate help. Two options for the short term are:

Call a meeting of your department and discuss sexual harassment. Tell your employees that Filmore Trust and you will not tolerate any behavior that is sexual in nature, unwelcome, or unreasonably disruptive.

Find an expert on sexual harassment who doesn't have any ties to Filmore Trust and give his or her name to Jill. Obviously, Jill doesn't trust the way your company would handle a sexual harassment complaint. Perhaps she might have greater confidence in advice coming from someone on the outside.

In the meantime, let Jill know your concerns but don't dismiss hers. The unfortunate truth is that a sexual harassment victim who makes a formal complaint to management without the protection of an established, trusted complaint procedure risks losing his or her reputation, job, or even career.

I know. When I brought my complaint to senior management, one of my greatest fears was retaliation. I wrote a letter, just like the one you are suggesting Jill write. In response, management thanked me for bringing sexual harassment to its attention and told me not to worry. I was promised it would be "business as usual" around the department.

But it wasn't. Instead of starting an investigation of my harasser, management started an investigation of me. It stole positive performance reviews out of my employee file and then told me my work was unsatisfactory because there weren't any good reviews on record. Colleagues who had once been sympathetic now didn't want to get involved. Others just stopped talking to me. Conversation would halt when I entered a room. So I sympathize with Jill when she wonders who will want to work with her if she brings a complaint. The answer often is no one.

And don't think that "nobody here has to find out." Long after I left my company, I heard that people were gossiping about the financial settlement I had received—and this in spite of a gag order.

Like other victims of sexual harassment, Jill hopes that the problem will eventually go away. Unfortunately, sexual harassment doesn't stop on its own. It simply goes somewhere else, finds someone else— unless people like you step in.

MARY P. ROWE

People who feel harassed need options and choices—especially if they lack conclusive proof of the harassment. This case appears to present two unacceptable choices for manager Jerry Tarkwell and no desirable options for Jill McNair. Moreover, Filmore Trust's policy will not work in the company's interests either. No party's interests are served well here.

Let's start with the company. Filmore Trust needs an environment where sexual harassment is absent or at least rare. This will occur where employees can and do speak up and get incipient harassment stopped on the spot, where managers offer options so people who feel harassed have some control over what happens, and where reporting harassment and asking for help will not damage someone's career.

My research and experience indicate that while a mandatory investigation policy may appear to be helpful to harassed people, it actually discourages reports of harassment. Mandatory investigation especially threatens careers when the only evidence is "he said/she said" (though more evidence might be found in the Filmore Trust case). This is because responsible managers hate to take action in such a case, so no one gets punished, and the alleged offender does not feel truly acquitted.

What about McNair's interests? They are the same interests I listed for Filmore Trust. In addition, McNair values her privacy and fears reprisal. Tarkwell's interests are probably similar.

How can Filmore Trust meet the interests of all parties? The company should offer four sets of options for dealing with harassment:

1. *Counseling for Direct Negotiation.* Filmore Trust should offer off-the-record counseling so that employees can learn to negotiate the problem effectively. With the help of an employee assistance program or an ombudsman, for example, McNair might choose to learn how to confront the harasser directly and/or write that person a private letter. Drafting a clear, factual letter will help McNair think through her evidence, compose her mind and feelings, and help her select and pursue an option for action. Sending or hand delivering (and keeping a copy of) a letter is statistically likely to end the harassment, at no cost to privacy. It also provides more evidence, if harassment continues or the offender retaliates, that the alleged sexual approach actually happened and was unwelcome.

2. *Informal, Third-Party Intervention.* McNair should be able to seek informal assistance from a human resource manager or other appropriate person. The third party would intervene as a shuttle diplomat or mediator. Informal intervention usually does not include adverse administrative action. The third party could deliver a warning and write a memo to his or her own file.

3. *Formal Investigation and Action.* McNair should be able to request fact-finding and judgment. If she knows she has choices, she will be more likely to make a formal complaint, but this option should not be pursued against her wishes.

4. *Generic Approach.* McNair should be able to ask Tarkwell or another appropriate manager—off the record and without providing the name of the alleged offender—for a harassment prevention effort. This choice could trigger an apparently routine training program in the relevant department. Or McNair could ask that the department head send a departmental letter that includes examples of sexual harassment and a strong statement of company policy. If McNair has the option to ask for such action without anyone's name being used, then the harassment can be stopped at no cost to anyone's privacy or rights. In my experience, the generic approach will stop the alleged harassment about four-fifths of the time, and it helps to affirm company policy. It also fosters an atmosphere where people can feel comfortable taking a direct approach if they are harassed and where they will feel less afraid to ask for an investigation.

There should be no adverse administrative action against an alleged offender without a fair—probably formal—process. If any of the informal options are chosen by McNair, then Tarkwell must follow up immediately, several months, and one year later to be sure that the alleged harassment has ceased and that there has been no retaliation.

MIKIKO TAGA

Jerry Tarkwell does not have to choose between respecting Jill McNair's privacy and putting a stop to sexual harassment. His accidental knowledge of McNair's harassment has given him, whether he likes it or not, the responsibility to do both.

It would be irresponsible to follow blindly "company policy" if to do so would undermine its original intent (presumably to help employees deal with harassment). Doing nothing, however, is also not an option. Sexual harassment involves the entire company, not just two people. Tarkwell therefore cannot let the issue go now that he knows something is going on.

As long as McNair refuses to report her case, Tarkwell will, by definition, be threatening her privacy in any attempts to talk to her about it. But McNair has already crossed the line between private and company life by using company equipment (e-mail) to tell her colleague about her sexual harassment. While Tarkwell must urge McNair to report her case, he must refrain from reporting it to the company's EEO until she assents.

Regardless of whether or not McNair ultimately reports her case, Tarkwell must make this his opportunity to attack the problem of sexual harassment and to raise company consciousness about it. Anything less would be shirking his responsibility of creating a safe working environment for his staff.

In Japan, on the other hand, a Jerry Tarkwell would have no cause to even mention his knowledge of Jill McNair's case to her, and the ethical problem presented by this situation would not have surfaced. Few Japanese companies have any sexual harassment policy in place.

Indeed, consciousness of sexual harassment here is so undeveloped that the very issue of the protection of privacy has yet to surface. For women, Japanese companies are still hotbeds of harassment.

The first sexual harassment suit filed in Japan was in 1989. The woman, who was being harassed by her immediate supervisor, complained to his boss, only to find that his boss condoned his actions and blamed her for inviting them. In other words, the men stuck together.

Within such a context, a woman must go beyond those immediately involved in order to be heard. But once she does, the rest of the company eventually finds out, she is further harassed, and, generally, she ends up quitting.

If she does file suit, she will most likely do so more out of a desire for revenge than of a feeling that her rights have been violated. Japan has such a long history of male dominance that there is no collective belief that a woman should be the equal working partner of a man.

I endured two years of sexual harassment—though at the time I did not know the term—while I was employed at a large manufacturing company. The older female employees taught the younger women that it was a mark of "female maturity" to respond to harassment by smiling and ignoring it.

During my stay in the United States (1983 to 1988), I was shocked to learn that there was a name for such hateful behavior. In 1989, when I published my book *Single Mind*, I was able to introduce the term sexual harassment to Japan.

In the three years since, the term *seku hara* has gained currency as the media has legitimized its usage. (In fact, seku hara is a trivialization of the term sexual harassment, further proof of the widespread insensitivity to this issue.) There have been three sexual harassment suits filed in Japan that I have followed; two have been won, and the other is still pending. Though this sounds promising, and though anti-seku hara campaigns would seem to indicate substantial change, the situation is, in fact, far from progressive. In effect, the message is "Watch out, guys. We know women are emotional, so we will have to step lightly for our own protection."

Ultimately, sexual harassment is less an issue of company policy than one of personal responsibility in a management position. Tarkwell has shown that he takes the company's policy seriously; now he should follow through on his commitment by ensuring that McNair's situation is justly resolved and by raising office consciousness about harassment.

JUDITH P. VLADECK

Jerry Tarkwell should respect Jill McNair's request for privacy. She is not obliged by law to press charges of harassment and should not be required to do so against her own better judgment. McNair is probably realistic about the potential damage to her career. She has no doubt seen the lack of sympathy and support available to a woman who complains about harassment. She should not be pressured into becoming an unwilling martyr.

If Tarkwell is concerned about McNair's complaining later that she was not protected by the company, he could ask her to provide a memo stating that she had considered her options and rejected the company's offer of assistance. If she declines to provide such a memo, Tarkwell should write his own memo to that effect and place it in McNair's personnel file. It would likely protect the company in the future.

Tarkwell, having alerted the EEO of his knowledge that a company employee was imposing on other workers, is in the difficult position of any good citizen who learns of a malfeasant in his community. If the victim refuses to press charges, the bystander cannot do so. Having encouraged the victim to do what he thinks is correct, he must accept her decision.

Obviously, a conscientious person such as Tarkwell could suggest that the company's harassment policy, with assurances of confidentiality, be circulated and posted again.

Whether McNair can be disciplined for refusing to cooperate in an investigation is a more difficult question. While reporting harassment is protected by law and retaliation against a person who does so violates federal law, failing to report is *not* protected by any clear statutory language. It might be argued that discipline for failing to report is a form of discrimination in itself. A woman who is required to report sexual harassment is being deprived of equal terms and conditions of employment, in that, unlike the men who are not subjected to the harassment, she is burdened with an obligation to come forward and place herself at risk.

Unfortunately, in many jurisdictions, a woman in McNair's position is at risk of discipline or termination for failing to disclose information requested by the company. In New York, for example, an employer who fired McNair for remaining silent could do so with impunity.

A subsidiary question arises concerning Tarkwell's conduct. If Tarkwell had not looked at McNair's computer screen, he would not have known about the problem. While it may be understandable that Tarkwell went into her office while she was not there to look for documents that he needed at once, his reading of her electronic mail message was inappropriate and an invasion of her privacy. McNair, unfortunately, has no right to the privacy of her personal e-mail, unless the company has some rules protecting the privacy rights of its employees.

Jill McNair is in the unenviable position of a woman trying to make a career for herself, who is likely to get battered for not publicly fighting back against the sexual harassment she is suffering and who risks ostracism and abuse from her colleagues if she does complain.

LEE CHESTER GARRON

Like many companies, Digital doesn't deny that sexual harassment exists in the workplace. Digital encourages managers and employees to take advantage of sexual harassment training, which examines the issue and develops solutions to harassment in any given work situation.

At Digital, 90% of all sexual harassment claims involve individuals who are not aware that their behaviors are offensive or unwelcome. And 90% of these claims are settled by an apology and a promise by the harasser to correct permanently his or her behavior. The remaining 10% might be settled with some disciplinary action.

A great deal of consideration should be given to validating any claim of sexual harassment, even before a full-fledged investigation takes place. This allows for the possibility that an employee might be filing a claim to offset poor performance or getting revenge for a personal relationship "gone sour." Evidence must be secured to avoid a "his word against mine" situation.

In the case of Jerry Tarkwell and Jill McNair, Tarkwell did exactly what I would recommend by first contacting Filmore Trust's EEO for instructions. Even though McNair demands that no further steps be taken, Tarkwell should continue to consult with the company EEO so a decision can be made about how to react to McNair's requests for anonymity. Only there can it be determined if the potential harm to the victim or other employees outweighs the complainant's concern for privacy. Tarkwell is responsible for acting on any issues that affect his employees, so McNair's situation cannot be ignored. At Digital, Tarkwell would be held accountable for his employees' behavior.

Tarkwell must pursue the issue, first to find out if the complaint is merited and then to ensure that no other incidents of harassment occur. Tarkwell can suggest that McNair seek the advice of another manager if she feels uncomfortable talking about it with him, and he must convince her that a company policy exists that will protect her. Every company's sexual harassment policy must contain a "no retaliation" stipulation promising that the complainant will not incur any kind of reprisal as a result of a claim.

Programs and policies assuring employees of their right to bring forth, without reprisal, issues that they feel are affecting them negatively are paramount to any positive or reasonable resolution in issues of sexual harassment. Many cases are resolved with simple, positive intervention—when the offended employee is convinced that the company will stand behind its policies, standards, and values. Helping employees understand not only their right to utilize the internal open-door process but also federal EEOC guidelines on sexual harassment and their right to use these avenues to find a resolution is very important. The prevention of sexual harassment in the workplace is the employer's responsibility.

To implement this policy successfully, Digital managers and supervisors are encouraged to know their environment and subordinates— as well as raise their level of awareness through sexual harassment training courses. The training involves role playing of actual sexual harassment situations and lively follow-up discussion in which attendees share their thoughts and ideas about the implications of sexual harassment. Digital's EEO also offers "Train the Trainer" seminars for human resource professionals to learn more about the issue and prepare them to train others. Digital's goal is to bring resolution to a sexual harassment claim and ensure the investigative process satisfies both the employee and management.

Note

Cheryl Wang, a former investment banker, is now a public television producer in New England. Mary P. Rowe is special assistant to the president, ombudsman, and adjunct professor at the Sloan School of Management at Massachusetts Institute of Technology. Mikiko Taga is a freelance journalist in Japan who writes about women's and other issues. Judity P. Vladeck is senior partner at Vladeck, Waldman, Elias & Engelhard, Counsellors at Law in New York City. Lee Chester Garron is equal employment officer/affirmative action training manager for Digital Equipment Corporation in Maynard, Massachusetts.

3

The Memo Every Woman Keeps in Her Desk

Kathleen Reardon

What kind of advice was I going to give Liz Ames, my pal from the good old days when we worked together in market development at Vision Software? Liz and I had been through a lot together, from working for an egomaniac who was finally fired to laying the groundwork for the biggest product launch in the company's history. We always seemed to understand each other's thoughts, and those Friday nights unwinding at the tavern made it possible for both of us to face work again Monday morning. We both had come a long way at Vision, and we were genuinely glad to see the other succeed. When I got the marketing director position in Germany, Liz was the first to congratulate me.

When we met for dinner the first night of the annual marketing retreat, I was ready to tell Liz all about my first six months on the new job, but she made it clear from the start that she had something urgent to discuss. She needed me to help her out of a dilemma, and she said my perspective as a man would be helpful. She had written a memo to John Clark, Vision's CEO, complaining about sexism at the company. Now she was agonizing over whether to send it. Liz seldom raised the subject of sexism, but she had written the memo because she thought it was time that someone at the top knew what was really going on at the company—in the trenches, as she put it.

She had no doubt that the message was important. But she did have doubts about how it would be received and about the fate of the messenger. She wanted me, her most trusted friend at Vision and a man, to help her decide what to do.

"In an ideal world," she said, "I wouldn't have any second thoughts about sending it. But you know what can happen to messengers. If Clark likes what I have to say, there's no problem. But then, there are the other possibilities."

"You've never been afraid to speak your mind. What's the worst that could happen?" I asked.

"Clark isn't going to fire me, if that's what you mean. But I can think of several ways this thing could backfire. What if Clark doesn't believe me, or he just can't relate to what I'm saying? He'll dismiss me as a radical feminist or a chronic complainer. Word will get around, and my career at Vision will be over. Or maybe he won't respond at all. It'll be one more example of not being heard. I don't know if I have the mental energy for that."

At first I thought Liz was being melodramatic, but as we talked I could see that to her, the decision was a turning point. She knew that ultimately she had to take responsibility for whatever decision she made, but she wanted my perspective. Reluctantly, I promised to use the memo as bedtime reading and get back to her in the morning. So there I sat with the memo in my lap, the hotel lamp glaring off the neatly typed pages.

> To: Mr. John Clark, CEO
> From: Elizabeth C. Ames, Director of Consumer Marketing
> Date: March 8, 1993
>
> I've been working in the marketing department at Vision Software for more than ten years, where I've had my share of challenges and successes. I've enjoyed being part of an interesting and exciting company. Despite my general enthusiasm about the company and my job, however, I was taken aback when I received your memo announcing the resignations of Mariam Blackwell and Susan French, Vision's two most senior women. This is not the first time Vision has lost its highest ranking women. Just nine months ago, Kathryn Hobbs resigned, and a year before that, it was Suzanne LaHaise. The reasons are surprisingly similar: they wanted to "spend more time with their families" or "explore new career directions."
>
> I can't help but detect a disturbing pattern. Why do such capable, conscientious women who have demonstrated intense commitment to their careers suddenly want to change course or spend more time at home? It's a question I've thought long and hard about.
>
> Despite Vision's policies to hire and promote women and your own efforts to recognize and reward women's contributions, the overall atmosphere in this company is one that slowly erodes a woman's sense of worth and place. I believe that top-level women are leaving Vision Soft-

ware not because they are drawn to other pursuits but because they are tired of struggling against a climate of female failure. Little things that happen daily—things many men don't even notice and women can't help but notice—send subtle messages that women are less important, less talented, less likely to make a difference than their male peers.

Let me try to describe what I mean. I'll start with meetings, which are a way of life at Vision and one of the most devaluing experiences for women. Women are often talked over and interrupted; their ideas never seem to be heard. Last week, I attended a meeting with ten men and one other woman. As soon as the woman started her presentation, several side conversations began. Her presentation skills were excellent, but she couldn't seem to get people's attention. When it was time to take questions, one man said dismissively, "We did something like this a couple of years ago, and it didn't work." She explained how her ideas differed, but the explanation fell on deaf ears. When I tried to give her support by expressing interest, I was interrupted.

But it's not just meetings. There are many things that make women feel unwelcome or unimportant. One department holds its biannual retreats at a country club with a "men only" bar. At the end of the sessions, the men typically hang around at the bar and talk, while the women quietly disappear. Needless to say, important information is often shared during those casual conversations.

Almost every formal meeting is followed by a series of informal ones behind closed doors. Women are rarely invited. Nor are they privy to the discussions before the formal meetings. As a result, they are often less likely to know what the boss has on his mind and therefore less prepared to react.

My female colleagues and I are also subjected to a daily barrage of seemingly innocent comments that belittle women. A coworker of mine recently boasted about how much he respects women by saying, "My wife is the wind beneath my wings. In fact, some people call me Mr. Karen Snyder." The men chuckled; the women didn't. And just last week, a male colleague stood up at 5:30 and jokingly informed a group of us that he would be leaving early: "I have to play mom tonight." Women play mom every night, and it never gets a laugh. In fact, most women try to appear devoid of concern about their families.

Any one of these incidents on its own is a small thing. But together and in repetition, they are quite powerful. The women at Vision fight to get their ideas heard and to crack the informal channels of information. Their energy goes into keeping up, not getting ahead, until they just don't have any more to give.

I can assure you that my observations are shared by many women in the company. I can only speculate that they were shared by Mariam Blackwell and Susan French.

Vision needs men and women if it is to become the preeminent educational software company. We need to send stronger, clearer signals that men are not the only people who matter. And this kind of change can work only if it starts with strong commitment at the top. That's why I'm writing to you. If I can be of help, please let me know.

Liz's memo seemed reasonable and compelling. Wouldn't Clark be grateful to hear from someone in the trenches? He liked to boast about the company's progressive policies toward diversity, and this would give him a chance to renew the crusade. He'd respect Liz for taking his commitment seriously.

But then again, Clark had an ego. Maybe he'd resent the implication that the company is not what he professes it to be. And, of course, it wasn't John Clark whom Liz had to face every day. Not all of Liz's male colleagues would give her criticisms any credence. And if they heard that she was writing to the boss complaining about them, they would shut her out. I had to admit, I could imagine that happening.

Did the consequences of sending the memo really matter? Wasn't there a principle involved? I knew that the stonewalling Liz had referred to was real. I'd witnessed it myself over the years. Liz was one of the most positive and energetic people I knew, but I remember several times when she was so strung out from having to prove herself to men who constantly challenged her authority that she was ready to quit. That would have been a serious loss of experience. She knew how to work with educators better than anyone I knew, and her impeccable follow-up was largely responsible for the success of the Vision II product line that now represents 20% of Vision's revenues.

But men were under pressure too. Maybe it just took a different form. Vision was a tough place, and marketing was the toughest department. Many times, I was tempted to pack it in myself. I'd seen a lot of men fail and a lot of women succeed at Vision. Take Mariam Blackwell. She fit Vision's corporate culture like a glove. If she wasn't heard the first time, she'd say it again. I think she left because she ran out of challenges, not because her psychic energy had been depleted. Susan French left because they gave her a V.P. title but removed the decision-making authority of her male predecessors—something Liz had not mentioned in her memo.

As I wrestled with the issues Liz raised, I realized that her dilemma had become a dilemma for me. If I advised Liz to send the memo, was I being naive about the consequences she might suffer? If I told her not to send it, was I somehow condoning the behavior she described? If I suggested that women were not the only ones who were sometimes run aground by Vision's demanding environment, was I being insensitive? If I don't buy into it, does that mean that I just don't get it?

What would I tell Liz?

Should Liz Send the Memo?

Experts discuss issues women face in the workplace.

RICHARD D. GLOVSKY

I would advise Liz not to send the memo at this time. A vigilant CEO would not have permitted this kind of discriminatory work environment to evolve in the first place. In short, the issues with which Liz is concerned would not exist at Vision unless Clark tacitly allowed them to develop. Clark cannot be trusted with Liz's message.

Instead of sending it, Liz should marshal her resources. She should speak with Mariam Blackwell, Susan French, Kathryn Hobbs, and Suzanne LaHaise to ascertain whether they have similar observations and would support her publicly. Liz also should talk to other women at Vision who can be trusted to maintain her confidence.

She should not "go it alone," especially when addressing a man more likely to be unreceptive than sympathetic. If Liz can get support (and statements) from other women who will corroborate her claims, she may be able to force Clark to do what is proper: review the employment environment at Vision and address Liz's issues on a company-wide basis.

Finally, if Liz decides to take her message to Clark, she should either see him in person with as many other credible colleagues as she can collect or send a memo signed by several Vision employees.

At a meeting, she should not be the only person to speak. Liz and her colleagues should divide the presentation so that no one person is the messenger. Clark will have a tendency to be vengeful and will focus on the leader of the group.

Unfortunately, because Clark may not react positively to the memo, Liz must use a more calculated and broad-based approach.

PHILIP A. MARINEAU

My advice is to send the memo. Sure, it's a risk. But not sending it will lead only to greater frustration—and eventually Liz will resign anyway. Chances are the CEO is already alarmed about the loss of his top two women executives and is wondering what he can do to prevent others from leaving. If he's smart, he'll not only listen to Liz's concerns but also make her a part of the search for solutions.

It's been my experience that listening to bright, committed employees throughout the company—regardless of gender, race, or level of experience—is one of the most important aspects of my job. It's the best way for me to identify situations that need more resources or attention from management.

Working with Quaker's Diversity Council, which includes staff members from a variety of demographic backgrounds and represents all divisions and levels, I have come to realize that pursuing traditional methods of developing future managers will not itself increase diversity significantly at the highest levels.

I am convinced that in order to ensure a better future, changes must begin with those at the top of the corporation. We've created a task force whose charge is to develop specific recommendations for ways in which Quaker can identify, nurture, retain, and advance women and minority executives. To make this work, we will have to set measurable goals, carefully and continuously monitor our progress, reward those managers who successfully carry out this mandate, and penalize those who don't. As a consumer products company, our guiding marketing principle is to stay close to our customers. To be successful, our internal policies and the makeup of our top management must reflect this principle as well. In the best interests of their company's future, Vision Software's senior executives should follow suit.

JOLINE GODFREY

Over the last twenty years, the percentage of women business owners has grown from 5% to over 30% and is still rising. By the end of

1992, more people will work in companies owned by women than will work in the *Fortune* 500. Liz helps us see why. If the dinosaur won't change, it will become extinct.

After years of banging heads against glass ceilings, huge numbers of women are realizing that learning how to dress, getting the right degrees, and struggling to fit in are essentially fruitless exercises. Of a certain age and self-awareness, women who are weary of trying to adapt to environments in which they are not welcome are leaving to create companies that fit them. The woman who feels strongly enough to write a memo is in the process of breaking with an unfriendly culture. Whether she sends it or not is unimportant—the process of alienation has begun. And if she chooses not to spend another calorie of energy teaching lessons that companies have had over two decades to learn—and are in their own best interests—that is her prerogative.

In fact, the Harvard Business School itself has documented the case of a woman whose ideas were rejected as "not workable" in a corporation. She eventually left that company and went on to start not one, but two highly successful companies ("Ruth M. Owades," HBS 9-383-051, revised February 1985). Tired of sending memos and sounding alarms, women are taking charge of their lives. What the leadership of the company does to address its workforce challenges will spell the survival or extinction of the company, regardless of whether Liz's memo is ever sent.

JAY M. JACKMAN

As any good mountaineer will tell you, a successful ascent requires a good deal of preparation: choosing fellow climbers, ensuring team conditioning, assembling first-rate equipment, and hiring experienced guides. Raising issues of sexism with the CEO of a corporation requires similar preparation. Liz definitely should discuss the issues of gender stonewalling at Vision Software with Clark but not alone, not yet, and not by memo.

Liz should not underestimate the difficulty of the mountain she has set out to climb. The undermining of women in the workplace is both common and difficult to change. It stems from a complicated interaction of men's beliefs and behaviors, women's beliefs and behaviors, the structures and procedures set up by companies, and the ways in which we organize and run our families. That the behaviors Liz cites have gone on for at least ten years without the CEO's notice (hardly an uncommon situation) underscores the difficulty of change. At the moment, the CEO is part of the problem; Liz's task is to make him part of the solution—no mean feat.

Liz needs to assemble allies: other women in the company, perhaps even some who have left, possibly certain members of the board, or men in the company. Singlehandedly attempting to change Clark's views is as foolhardy as attempting a solo alpine ascent. Also, Liz needs to strengthen the case to be presented to Clark. She needs more than the "anecdotes" she cites in her memo and must give Clark concrete reasons why women are leaving the company, not just speculation.

Liz also must talk with experts. There are many academics and consultants who help women and companies understand the dynamics behind sexist practices and work with them toward change. Successfully approaching a CEO about alleviating sexism—a process that ultimately will require major changes in corporate culture and structure—needs expert guidance.

Finally, we would urge Liz, with one or two people from the group she assembles, to talk to Clark in person rather than sending a memo. At the moment, she has no idea where he stands on the subject of sexism. In a meeting, she can observe when he gets defensive, test his willingness to cooperate, and suggest incremental changes that he is likely to back. Women with ten years of experience in a corporation are precious assets; as they move to improve the system for women in general, they should not sacrifice themselves.

Liz Ames's dilemma raises a larger issue that permeates corporate life: How is it that we have created institutions in which people are afraid to express the truth as they see it? *Bhopal, Three Mile Island, and the Ford Pinto all were preceded by memos unsent or unread.*

Vision Software is losing out because it operates in a culture of exclusion. The company has suffered and will continue to suffer, both internally and in the marketplace, because it refuses to look clearly at itself. If it cannot intelligently reveal its own inner workings in a way that is collaborative and supportive of its members, then it defies its own mission to produce educational software. The company's mission, and Liz's challenge, is to absorb information from the environment and incorporate that information into an evolving system, whether it be a human being or a corporation—that is what learning is all about.

If we are to re-create our corporate organizations so that they become more socially and environmentally responsible, business will have to learn from nature. All living systems depend on constant feedback loops that recalibrate the organism's relationship to life around it. Vision's corporate culture appears to accept only feedback loops that reinforce maladaptive behavior such as sexist or exclusionary practices.

For that reason Liz has to send her memo. Her career, after all, does depend on it. Maybe not her career within the context of Vision Software—particularly if it is read in an unsympathetic light—but her life goal. Liz has to remember that she set out not only to bring home a paycheck but also to express her own values and qualities in the commercial arena.

If she doesn't file the memo, Liz will be left with the new dilemma of subordinating her own wisdom and sense of self to a system that is not fully functional. She will have an aborted sense of her own value, an acute loss in a world that is crying out for more value to be added to it. If business is about adding value, then what better place to find it than within ourselves.

GLORIA STEINEM

Unless Liz is in imminent danger of hunger or homelessness, I would advise her to send the memo. If she doesn't, she is not only acting against her own and other women's long-term interest but also failing to give her company her best advice.

With that in mind, I would also change the memo's tone. Right now, it has a tone of apology and includes no reference at all to the company's goals. Liz should make a case for Vision Software to choose a self-interested path toward inclusiveness for the long-term benefit of the company's employees—and its bottom line.

I would advise her to write the memo with the same enthusiasm she would express if she were telling her boss about a new technology that could put Vision ahead of its competitors. Because that is exactly what she's doing: discovering a new technology. Just because it's a "soft" technology of human resources rather than one relating to inanimate objects doesn't mean her discoveries are less important. Indeed, they may be further-reaching and more important. Liz can underscore this by using such "hard" facts as company and industry-wide statistics on the cost of losing a trained executive. The goal here is to help the boss see his female employees' problems as his own and thus their solution as his victory. Empathy is the most revolutionary emotion.

What's interesting about this case study, however, is that Liz's male colleague never raises the question of whether he should cosign the memo. Or whether he should offer to support it with one of his own. Or whether he might join her in asking one or more supportive colleagues—male or female—to become part of this process.

These unaddressed options are symbolic of the ways in which sexism is regarded as the problem of women—just as racism is regarded as the problem of people of color—when in fact, those problems limit everyone. Until the more powerful own the responsibility for prejudice, it will continue to cripple us all.

Note

Richard D. Glovsky is the former chief of the Civil Division of the United States Attorney's Office in Boston and founder of Boston-based Glovsky & Associates. Philip A. Marineau is executive vice president and chief operating officer at the Quaker Oats Company. Jay M. Jackman, M.D., is a private-practice psychiatrist and a consultant for organizational change. Myra H. Strober is a labor economist at the School of Education at Stanford University and a consultant on issues of employment of women and minorities. Joline Godfrey is the founder and director of An Income of Her Own, a company that specializes in entrepreneurial education for teenage women. Paul Hawken is the founder of Smith & Hawken, a catalog company known for its environmental initiatives, but is no longer affiliated with the company. Gloria Steinem is a founder and consulting editor of *Ms. Magazine*.

PART

III

The Balancing Act

1
Management Women and the New Facts of Life

Felice N. Schwartz

The cost of employing women in management is greater than the cost of employing men. This is a jarring statement, partly because it is true, but mostly because it is something people are reluctant to talk about. A new study by one multinational corporation shows that the rate of turnover in management positions is 2-1/2 times higher among top-performing women than it is among men. A large producer of consumer goods reports that one half of the women who take maternity leave return to their jobs late or not at all. And we know that women also have a greater tendency to plateau or to interrupt their careers in ways that limit their growth and development. But we have become so sensitive to charges of sexism and so afraid of confrontation, even litigation, that we rarely say what we know to be true. Unfortunately, our bottled-up awareness leaks out in misleading metaphors ("glass ceiling" is one notable example), veiled hostility, lowered expectations, distrust, and reluctant adherence to Equal Employment Opportunity requirements.

Career interruptions, plateauing, and turnover are expensive. The money corporations invest in recruitment, training, and development is less likely to produce top executives among women than among men, and the invaluable company experience that developing executives acquire at every level as they move up through management ranks is more often lost.

The studies just mentioned are only the first of many, I'm quite sure. Demographic realities are going to force corporations all across the country to analyze the cost of employing women in managerial positions, and what they will discover is that women cost more.

But here is another startling truth: The greater cost of employing women is not a function of inescapable gender differences. Women *are* different from men, but what increases their cost to the corporation is principally the clash of their perceptions, attitudes, and behavior with those of men, which is to say, with the policies and practices of male-led corporations.

It is terribly important that employers draw the right conclusions from the studies now being done. The studies will be useless—or worse, harmful—if all they teach us is that women are expensive to employ. What we need to learn is how to reduce that expense, how to stop throwing away the investments we make in talented women, how to become more responsive to the needs of the women that corporations *must* employ if they are to have the best and the brightest of all those now entering the work force.

The gender differences relevant to business fall into two categories: those related to maternity and those related to the differing traditions and expectations of the sexes. Maternity is biological rather than cultural. We can't alter it, but we can dramatically reduce its impact on the workplace and in many cases eliminate its negative effect on employee development. We can accomplish this by addressing the second set of differences, those between male and female socialization. Today, these differences exaggerate the real costs of maternity and can turn a relatively slight disruption in work schedule into a serious business problem and a career derailment for individual women. If we are to overcome the cost differential between male and female employees, we need to address the issues that arise when female socialization meets the male corporate culture and masculine rules of career development—issues of behavior and style, of expectation, of stereotypes and preconceptions, of sexual tension and harassment, of female mentoring, lateral mobility, relocation, compensation, and early identification of top performers.

The one immutable, enduring difference between men and women is maternity. Maternity is not simply childbirth but a continuum that begins with an awareness of the ticking of the biological clock, proceeds to the anticipation of motherhood, includes pregnancy, childbirth, physical recuperation, psychological adjustment, and continues on to nursing, bonding, and child rearing. Not all women choose to become mothers, of course, and among those who do, the process varies from case to case depending on the health of the mother and baby, the values of the parents, and the availability, cost, and quality of child care.

In past centuries, the biological fact of maternity shaped the traditional roles of the sexes. Women performed the home-centered functions that related to the bearing and nurturing of children. Men did the work that required great physical strength. Over time, however, family size contracted, the community assumed greater responsibility for the care and education of children, packaged foods and household technology reduced the work load in the home, and technology eliminated much of the need for muscle power at the workplace. Today, in the developed world, the only role still uniquely gender related is childbearing. Yet men and women are still socialized to perform their traditional roles.

Men and women may or may not have some innate psychological disposition toward these traditional roles—men to be aggressive, competitive, self-reliant, risk taking; women to be supportive, nurturing, intuitive, sensitive, communicative—but certainly both men and women are capable of the full range of behavior. Indeed, the male and female roles have already begun to expand and merge. In the decades ahead, as the socialization of boys and girls and the experience and expectations of young men and women grow steadily more androgynous, the differences in workplace behavior will continue to fade. At the moment, however, we are still plagued by disparities in perception and behavior that make the integration of men and women in the workplace unnecessarily difficult and expensive.

Let me illustrate with a few broadbrush generalizations. Of course, these are only stereotypes, but I think they help to exemplify the kinds of preconceptions that can muddy the corporate waters.

Men continue to perceive women as the rearers of their children, so they find it understandable, indeed appropriate, that women should renounce their careers to raise families. Edmund Pratt, CEO of Pfizer, once asked me in all sincerity, "Why would any woman choose to be a chief financial officer rather than a full-time mother?" By condoning and taking pleasure in women's traditional behavior, men reinforce it. Not only do they see parenting as fundamentally female, they see a career as fundamentally male—either an unbroken series of promotions and advancements toward CEOdom or stagnation and disappointment. This attitude serves to legitimize a woman's choice to extend maternity leave and even, for those who can afford it, to leave employment altogether for several years. By the same token, men who might want to take a leave after the birth of a child know that management will see such behavior as a lack of career commitment, even when company policy permits parental leave for men.

Women also bring counterproductive expectations and perceptions to the workplace. Ironically, although the feminist movement was an expression of women's quest for freedom from their home-based lives, most women were remarkably free already. They had many responsibilities, but they were autonomous and could be entrepreneurial in how and when they carried them out. And once their children grew up and left home, they were essentially free to do what they wanted with their lives. Women's traditional role also included freedom from responsibility for the financial support of their families. Many of us were socialized from girlhood to expect our husbands to take care of us, while our brothers were socialized from an equally early age to complete their educations, pursue careers, climb the ladder of success, and provide dependable financial support for their families. To the extent that this tradition of freedom lingers subliminally, women tend to bring to their employment a sense that they can choose to change jobs or careers at will, take time off, or reduce their hours.

Finally, women's traditional role encouraged particular attention to the quality and substance of what they did, specifically to the physical, psychological, and intellectual development of their children. This traditional focus may explain women's continuing tendency to search for more than monetary reward—intrinsic significance, social importance, meaning—in what they do. This too makes them more likely than men to leave the corporation in search of other values.

The misleading metaphor of the glass ceiling suggests an invisible barrier constructed by corporate leaders to impede the upward mobility of women beyond the middle levels. A more appropriate metaphor, I believe, is the kind of cross-sectional diagram used in geology. The barriers to women's leadership occur when potentially counterproductive layers of influence on women—maternity, tradition, socialization—meet management strata pervaded by the largely unconscious preconceptions, stereotypes, and expectations of men. Such interfaces do not exist for men and tend to be impermeable for women.

One result of these gender differences has been to convince some executives that women are simply not suited to top management. Other executives feel helpless. If they see even a few of their valued female employees fail to return to work from maternity leave on schedule or see one of their most promising women plateau in her career after the birth of a child, they begin to fear there is nothing they can do to infuse women with new energy and enthusiasm and persuade them to stay. At the same time, they know there is nothing they can do to stem the tide of women into management ranks.

Another result is to place every working woman on a continuum that runs from total dedication to career at one end to a balance between career and family at the other. What women discover is that the male corporate culture sees both extremes as unacceptable. Women who want the flexibility to balance their families and their careers are not adequately committed to the organization. Women who perform as aggressively and competitively as men are abrasive and unfeminine. But the fact is, business needs all the talented women it can get. Moreover, as I will explain, the women I call career-primary and those I call career-and-family each have particular value to the corporation.

Women in the corporation are about to move from a buyer's to a seller's market. The sudden, startling recognition that 80% of new entrants in the work force over the next decade will be women, minorities, and immigrants has stimulated a mushrooming incentive to "value diversity."

Women are no longer simply an enticing pool of occasional creative talent, a thorn in the side of the EEO officer, or a source of frustration to corporate leaders truly puzzled by the slowness of their upward trickle into executive positions. A real demographic change is taking place. The era of sudden population growth of the 1950s and 1960s is over. The birth rate has dropped about 40%, from a high of 25.3 live births per 1,000 population in 1957, at the peak of the baby boom, to a stable low of a little more than 15 per 1,000 over the last 16 years, and there is no indication of a return to a higher rate. The tidal wave of baby boomers that swelled the recruitment pool to overflowing seems to have been a one-time phenomenon. For 20 years, employers had the pick of a very large crop and were able to choose males almost exclusively for the executive track. But if future population remains fairly stable while the economy continues to expand, and if the new information society simultaneously creates a greater need for creative, educated managers, then the gap between supply and demand will grow dramatically and, with it, the competition for managerial talent.

The decrease in numbers has even greater implications if we look at the traditional source of corporate recruitment for leadership positions—white males from the top 10% of the country's best universities. Over the past decade, the increase in the number of women graduating from leading universities has been much greater than the increase in the total number of graduates, and these women are well represented in the top 10% of their classes.

The trend extends into business and professional programs as well.

In the old days, virtually all MBAs were male. I remember addressing a meeting at the Harvard Business School as recently as the mid-1970s and looking out at a sea of exclusively male faces. Today, about 25% of that audience would be women. The pool of male MBAs from which corporations have traditionally drawn their leaders has shrunk significantly.

Of course, this reduction does not have to mean a shortage of talent. The top 10% is at least as smart as it always was—smarter, probably, since it's now drawn from a broader segment of the population. But it now consists increasingly of women. Companies that are determined to recruit the same number of men as before will have to dig much deeper into the male pool, while their competitors will have the opportunity to pick the best people from both the male and female graduates.

Under these circumstances, there is no question that the management ranks of business will include increasing numbers of women. There remains, however, the question of how these women will succeed—how long they will stay, how high they will climb, how completely they will fulfill their promise and potential, and what kind of return the corporation will realize on its investment in their training and development.

There is ample business reason for finding ways to make sure that as many of these women as possible will succeed. The first step in this process is to recognize that women are not all alike. Like men, they are individuals with differing talents, priorities, and motivations. For the sake of simplicity, let me focus on the two women I referred to earlier, on what I call the career-primary woman and the career-and-family woman.

Like many men, some women put their careers first. They are ready to make the same trade-offs traditionally made by the men who seek leadership positions. They make a career decision to put in extra hours, to make sacrifices in their personal lives, to make the most of every opportunity for professional development. For women, of course, this decision also requires that they remain single or at least childless or, if they do have children, that they be satisfied to have others raise them. Some 90% of executive men but only 35% of executive women have children by the age of 40. The *automatic* association of all women with babies is clearly unjustified.

The secret to dealing with such women is to recognize them early, accept them, and clear artificial barriers from their path to the top.

After all, the best of these women are among the best managerial talent you will ever see. And career-primary women have another important value to the company that men and other women lack. They can act as role models and mentors to younger women who put their careers first. Since upwardly mobile career-primary women still have few role models to motivate and inspire them, a company with women in its top echelon has a significant advantage in the competition for executive talent.

Men at the top of the organization—most of them over 55, with wives who tend to be traditional—often find career women "masculine" and difficult to accept as colleagues. Such men miss the point, which is not that these women are just like men but that they are just like the *best* men in the organization. And there is such a shortage of the best people that gender cannot be allowed to matter. It is clearly counterproductive to disparage in a woman with executive talent the very qualities that are most critical to the business and that might carry a man to the CEO's office.

Clearing a path to the top for career-primary women has four requirements:

1. Identify them early.
2. Give them the same opportunity you give to talented men to grow and develop and contribute to company profitability. Give them client and customer responsibility. Expect them to travel and relocate, to make the same commitment to the company as men aspiring to leadership positions.
3. Accept them as valued members of your management team. Include them in every kind of communication. Listen to them.
4. Recognize that the business environment is more difficult and stressful for them than for their male peers. They are always a minority, often the only woman. The male perception of talented, ambitious women is at best ambivalent, a mixture of admiration, resentment, confusion, competitiveness, attraction, skepticism, anxiety, pride, and animosity. Women can never feel secure about how they should dress and act, whether they should speak out or grin and bear it when they encounter discrimination, stereotyping, sexual harassment, and paternalism. Social interaction and travel with male colleagues and with male clients can be charged. As they move up, the normal increase in pressure and responsibility is compounded for women because they are women.

Stereotypical language and sexist day-to-day behavior do take their toll on women's career development. Few male executives realize how common it is to call women by their first names while men in the same group are greeted with surnames, how frequently female executives are assumed by men to be secretaries, how often women are excluded from all-male social events where business is being transacted. With notable exceptions, men are still generally more comfortable with other men, and as a result women miss many of the career and business opportunities that arise over lunch, on the golf course, or in the locker room.

The majority of women, however, are what I call career-and-family women, women who want to pursue serious careers while participating actively in the rearing of children. These women are a precious resource that has yet to be mined. Many of them are talented and creative. Most of them are willing to trade some career growth and compensation for freedom from the constant pressure to work long hours and weekends.

Most companies today are ambivalent at best about the career-and-family women in their management ranks. They would prefer that all employees were willing to give their all to the company. They believe it is in their best interests for all managers to compete for the top positions so the company will have the largest possible pool from which to draw its leaders.

"If you have both talent and motivation," many employers seem to say, "we want to move you up. If you haven't got that motivation, if you want less pressure and greater flexibility, then you can leave and make room for a new generation." These companies lose on two counts. First, they fail to amortize the investment they made in the early training and experience of management women who find themselves committed to family as well as to career. Second, they fail to recognize what these women could do for their middle management.

The ranks of middle managers are filled with people on their way up and people who have stalled. Many of them have simply reached their limits, achieved career growth commensurate with or exceeding their capabilities, and they cause problems because their performance is mediocre but they still want to move ahead. The career-and-family woman is willing to trade off the pressures and demands that go with promotion for the freedom to spend more time with her children. She's very smart, she's talented, she's committed to her career, and she's satisfied to stay at the middle level, at least during the early child-rearing years. Compare her with some of the people you have there now.

Consider a typical example, a woman who decides in college on a business career and enters management at age 22. For nine years, the company invests in her career as she gains experience and skills and steadily improves her performance. But at 31, just as the investment begins to pay off in earnest, she decides to have a baby. Can the company afford to let her go home, take another job, or go into business for herself? The common perception now is yes, the corporation can afford to lose her unless, after six or eight weeks or even three months of disability and maternity leave, she returns to work on a full-time schedule with the same vigor, commitment, and ambition that she showed before.

But what if she doesn't? What if she wants or needs to go on leave for six months or a year or, heaven forbid, five years? In this worst-case scenario, she works full-time from age 22 to 31 and from 36 to 65—a total of 38 years as opposed to the typical male's 43 years. That's not a huge difference. Moreover, my typical example is willing to work part-time while her children are young, if only her employer will give her the opportunity. There are two rewards for companies responsive to this need: higher retention of their best people and greatly improved performance and satisfaction in their middle management.

The high-performing career-and-family woman can be a major player in your company. She can give you a significant business advantage as the competition for able people escalates. Sometimes too, if you can hold on to her, she will switch gears in mid-life and re-enter the competition for the top. The price you must pay to retain these women is threefold: you must plan for and manage maternity, you must provide the flexibility that will allow them to be maximally productive, and you must take an active role in helping to make family supports and high-quality, affordable child care available to all women.

The key to managing maternity is to recognize the value of high-performing women and the urgent need to retain them and keep them productive. The first step must be a genuine partnership between the woman and her boss. I know this partnership can seem difficult to forge. One of my own senior executives came to me recently to discuss plans for her maternity leave and subsequent return to work. She knew she wanted to come back. I wanted to make certain that she would. Still, we had a somewhat awkward conversation, because I knew that no woman can predict with certainty when she will be able to return to work or under what conditions. Physical problems can lengthen her leave. So can a demanding infant, a difficult family or personal adjustment, or problems with child care.

I still don't know when this valuable executive will be back on the job full-time, and her absence creates some genuine problems for our organization. But I do know that I can't simply replace her years of experience with a new recruit. Since our conversation, I also know that she wants to come back, and that she *will* come back—part-time at first—unless I make it impossible for her by, for example, setting an arbitrary date for her full-time return or resignation. In turn, she knows that the organization wants and needs her and, more to the point, that it will be responsive to her needs in terms of working hours and child-care arrangements.

In having this kind of conversation it's important to ask concrete questions that will help to move the discussion from uncertainty and anxiety to some level of predictability. Questions can touch on everything from family income and energy level to child care arrangements and career commitment. Of course you want your star manager to return to work as soon as possible, but you want her to return permanently and productively. Her downtime on the job is a drain on her energies and a waste of your money.

For all the women who want to combine career and family—the women who want to participate actively in the rearing of their children and who also want to pursue their careers seriously—the key to retention is to provide the flexibility and family supports they need in order to function effectively.

Time spent in the office increases productivity if it is time well spent, but the fact that most women continue to take the primary responsibility for child care is a cause of distraction, diversion, anxiety, and absenteeism—to say nothing of the persistent guilt experienced by all working mothers. A great many women, perhaps most of all women who have always performed at the highest levels, are also frustrated by a sense that while their children are babies they cannot function at their best either at home or at work.

In its simplest form, flexibility is the freedom to take time off—a couple of hours, a day, a week—or to do some work at home and some at the office, an arrangement that communication technology makes increasingly feasible. At the complex end of the spectrum are alternative work schedules that permit the woman to work less than full-time and her employer to reap the benefits of her experience and, with careful planning, the top level of her abilities.

Part-time employment is the single greatest inducement to getting women back on the job expeditiously and the provision women themselves most desire. A part-time return to work enables them to maintain responsibility for critical aspects of their jobs, keeps them in touch with the changes constantly occurring at the workplace and in the job itself, reduces stress and fatigue, often eliminates the need for paid maternity leave by permitting a return to the office as soon as disability leave is over, and, not least, can greatly enhance company loyalty. The part-time solution works particularly well when a work load can be reduced for one individual in a department or when a full-time job can be broken down by skill levels and apportioned to two individuals at different levels of skill and pay.

I believe, however, that shared employment is the most promising and will be the most widespread form of flexible scheduling in the future. It is feasible at every level of the corporation except at the pinnacle, for both the short and the long term. It involves two people taking responsibility for one job.

Two red lights flash on as soon as most executives hear the words "job sharing": continuity and client-customer contact. The answer to the continuity question is to place responsibility entirely on the two individuals sharing the job to discuss everything that transpires—thoroughly, daily, and on their own time. The answer to the problem of client-customer contact is yes, job sharing requires reeducation and a period of adjustment. But as both client and supervisor will quickly come to appreciate, two contacts means that the customer has continuous access to the company's representative, without interruptions for vacation, travel, or sick leave. The two people holding the job can simply cover for each other, and the uninterrupted, full-time coverage they provide together can be a stipulation of their arrangement.

Flexibility is costly in numerous ways. It requires more supervisory time to coordinate and manage, more office space, and somewhat greater benefits costs (though these can be contained with flexible benefits plans, prorated benefits, and, in two-paycheck families, elimination of duplicate benefits). But the advantages of reduced turnover and the greater productivity that results from higher energy levels and greater focus can outweigh the costs.

A few hints:

Provide flexibility selectively. I'm not suggesting private arrangements subject to the suspicion of favoritism but rather a policy that makes flexible work schedules available only to high performers.

Make it clear that in most instances (but not all) the rates of advancement and pay will be appropriately lower for those who take time off or who work part-time than for those who work full-time. Most career-and-family women are entirely willing to make that trade-off.

Discuss costs as well as benefits. Be willing to risk accusations of bias. Insist, for example, that half time is half of whatever time it takes to do the job, not merely half of 35 or 40 hours.

The woman who is eager to get home to her child has a powerful incentive to use her time effectively at the office and to carry with her reading and other work that can be done at home. The talented professional who wants to have it all can be a high performer by carefully ordering her priorities and by focusing on objectives rather than on the legendary 15-hour day. By the time professional women have their first babies—at an average age of 31—they have already had nine years to work long hours at a desk, to travel, and to relocate. In the case of high performers, the need for flexibility coincides with what has gradually become the goal-oriented nature of responsibility.

Family supports—in addition to maternity leave and flexibility—include the provision of parental leave for men, support for two-career and single-parent families during relocation, and flexible benefits. But the primary ingredient is child care. The capacity of working mothers to function effectively and without interruption depends on the availability of good, affordable child care. Now that women make up almost half the work force and the growing percentage of managers, the decision to become involved in the personal lives of employees is no longer a philosophical question but a practical one. To make matters worse, the quality of child care has almost no relation to technology, inventiveness, or profitability but is more or less a pure function of the quality of child care personnel and the ratio of adults to children. These costs are irreducible. Only by joining hands with government and the public sector can corporations hope to create the vast quantity and variety of child care that their employees need.

Until quite recently, the response of corporations to women has been largely symbolic and cosmetic, motivated in large part by the will to avoid litigation and legal penalties. In some cases, companies were also moved by a genuine sense of fairness and a vague discomfort and frustration at the absence of women above the middle of the corporate pyramid. The actions they took were mostly quick, easy, and highly visible—child care information services, a three-month parental leave available to men as well as women, a woman appointed to the board of directors.

When I first began to discuss these issues 26 years ago, I was sometimes able to get an appointment with the assistant to the assistant in personnel, but it was only a courtesy. Over the past decade, I have met with the CEOs of many large corporations, and I've watched them become involved with ideas they had never previously thought much about. Until recently, however, the shelf life of that enhanced awareness was always short. Given pressing, short-term concerns, women were not a front-burner issue. In the past few months, I have seen yet another change. Some CEOs and top management groups now take the initiative. They call and ask us to show them how to shift gears from a responsive to a proactive approach to recruiting, developing, and retaining women.

I think this change is more probably a response to business needs—to concern for the quality of future profits and managerial talent—than to uneasiness about legal requirements, sympathy with the demands of women and minorities, or the desire to do what is right and fair. The nature of such business motivation varies. Some companies want to move women to higher positions as role models for those below them and as beacons for talented young recruits. Some want to achieve a favorable image with employees, customers, clients, and stockholders. These are all legitimate motives. But I think the companies that stand to gain most are motivated as well by a desire to capture competitive advantage in an era when talent and competence will be in increasingly short supply. These companies are now ready to stop being defensive about their experience with women and to ask incisive questions without preconceptions.

Even so, incredibly, I don't know of more than one or two companies that have looked into their own records to study the absolutely critical issue of maternity leave—how many women took it, when and whether they returned, and how this behavior correlated with their rank, tenure, age, and performance. The unique drawback to the employment of women is the physical reality of maternity and the particular socializing influence maternity has had. Yet to make women equal to men in the workplace we have chosen on the whole not to discuss this single most significant difference between them. Unless we do, we cannot evaluate the cost of recruiting, developing, and moving women up.

Now that interest is replacing indifference, there are four steps every company can take to examine its own experience with women:

1. Gather quantitative data on the company's experience with management-level women regarding turnover rates, occurrence of and return from maternity leave, and organizational level attained in relation to tenure and performance.
2. Correlate this data with factors such as age, marital status, and presence and age of children, and attempt to identify and analyze why women respond the way they do.
3. Gather qualitative data on the experience of women in your company and on how women are perceived by both sexes.
4. Conduct a cost-benefit analysis of the return on your investment in high-performing women. Factor in the cost to the company of women's negative reactions to negative experience, as well as the probable cost of corrective measures and policies. If women's value to your company is greater than the cost to recruit, train, and develop them—and of course I believe it will be—then you will want to do everything you can to retain them.

We have come a tremendous distance since the days when the prevailing male wisdom saw women as lacking the kind of intelligence that would allow them to succeed in business. For decades, even women themselves have harbored an unspoken belief that they couldn't make it because they couldn't be just like men, and nothing else would do. But now that women have shown themselves the equal of men in every area of organizational activity, now that they have demonstrated that they can be stars in every field of endeavor, now we can all venture to examine the fact that women and men are different.

On balance, employing women is more costly than employing men. Women can acknowledge this fact today because they know that their value to employers exceeds the additional cost and because they know that changing attitudes can reduce the additional cost dramatically. Women in management are no longer an idiosyncrasy of the arts and education. They have always matched men in natural ability. Within a very few years, they will equal men in numbers as well in every area of economic activity.

The demographic motivation to recruit and develop women is compelling. But an older question remains: Is society better for the change? Women's exit from the home and entry into the work force has certainly created problems—an urgent need for good, affordable child care; troubling questions about the kind of parenting children need; the costs and difficulties of diversity in the workplace; the stress and fatigue of combining work and family responsibilities. Wouldn't we all be happier if we could turn back the clock to an age when men were in the workplace and women in the home, when male and female roles were clearly differentiated and complementary?

Nostalgia, anxiety, and discouragement will urge many to say yes, but my answer is emphatically no. Two fundamental benefits that were unattainable in the past are now within our reach. For the individual, freedom of choice—in this case the freedom to choose career, family, or a combination of the two. For the corporation, access to the most gifted individuals in the country. These benefits are neither self-indulgent nor insubstantial. Freedom of choice and self-realization are too deeply American to be cast aside for some wistful vision of the past. And access to our most talented human resources is not a luxury in this age of explosive international competition but rather the barest minimum that prudence and national self-preservation require.

2
Mother's Work

Nan Stone

Women's Quest for Economic Equality
by Victor R. Fuchs
Cambridge: Harvard University Press, 1988
171 pages. $18.95.

The Second Shift
by Arlie Hochschild with Anne Machung
New York: Viking, 1989
308 pages. $18.95.

The controversy prompted by Felice Schwartz's "Management Women and the New Facts of Life" [Chapter 1, Part III, this volume] shows no sign of ending. More than half a year after the article's publication in HBR, the public is still heatedly debating the touchy subject Schwartz raised—women, maternity, and work. Now two important and thought-provoking books challenge us to expand the discussion once again. *Women's Quest for Economic Equality* studies working women in the aggregate, while *The Second Shift* gives us a more intimate view of individual working mothers' lives. But despite this difference in approach, both books make us confront the same uncomfortable question: What happens at home—to the family, to children—when both father and mother work full time?

Questions about the care of children might seem extraneous in a book called *Women's Quest for Economic Equality*. But for Victor Fuchs, a professor of economics and health research and policy at Stanford, the two subjects are inextricably intertwined. Drawing mostly on economic and demographic data from the U.S. Census Bureau, Fuchs argues that conflicts between family and career are the primary reason that women are still economically weaker than men. In the process, he challenges several common assumptions about the progress women have—and have not—made in the last quarter-century.

One of these assumptions is that for the most part, women are better off today than they were in 1960. Not so, says Fuchs. When you look at women's economic well-being (which includes not only money income but also the value of the goods and services produced at home and available leisure time as measured by hours free of paid and unpaid work), most women are about where they were in 1960, or they have fallen a little behind. The wage gap persists, although women's dollar income has risen. Women have less leisure time while men have more. Women are more dependent on their own income for support. Women's share of the financial responsibility for children has grown.

There is one exception to this general pattern. Young, white, unmarried, educated women have made great gains relative to their male peers. If, that is, they have no children. (Unmarried women as a category includes those who are divorced or widowed.) Women with children, to use Fuchs's phrase, "frequently live under great pressure."

What explains this persistent inequality? Discrimination is an obvious answer, and Fuchs repeatedly reminds us that it is a real and considerable barrier for many women at some time in their lives. But Fuchs contests the idea that discrimination and exploitation by employers is the primary reason for women's lack of progress. (Remember, he is talking about women in the aggregate, not individual cases.) Segregation by occupation and industry is too persistent and widespread. The wage gap remains too big. Burdens at home are too unequal. A more reasonable explanation, he suggests, has to do with women themselves, particularly the conflict they experience over their families and careers.

Fuchs locates the source of this conflict in the fact that *on average*, women want children more than men do and feel a greater concern for their well-being. To explain why women feel this bond, he draws on biology (albeit gingerly, since he recognizes how often biological explanations have been "misused to justify inequality") and on first-hand experiences of mothers. But his primary proof comes from statistics, among them figures on residential custody patterns (as compared with legal custody agreements) and on the large numbers of children born to and living with single mothers. One of the many unfamiliar statistics that Fuchs reports is that women over the age of

20 account for two-thirds of all births to single mothers. By his calculation, half these births are intended at the time of conception.

To accommodate their desire for children, women have typically made choices that curtailed their economic power. A "traditional" marriage in which husbands and wives inhabit separate spheres of work and home was—and still is—one of these choices. But as Fuchs points out, it is an option that fewer and fewer women are likely to have. The fundamental economic, demographic, and technological changes that have brought so many women into the workplace—the wide availability of service jobs, better birth control methods, the prevalence of divorce—work against the traditional marriage. So do changes in women's expectations for themselves, among them the expectation that they will participate equally in society by doing paid work.

Women have also held themselves back through erratic participation in the work force and the kinds of jobs they have traditionally prepared themselves for and taken. Many women work in occupations that do not require a great deal of training or technical skill, and they have been more likely to do part-time work or take full-time jobs that mesh with the needs of children (jobs with predictable hours, for example). Unfortunately, the freedom to leave work at 3 P.M.—or even at 5 P.M., without a bulging briefcase—is a costly trade-off if, like many women, you are barely making ends meet and are struggling mightily to give your children proper care.

To improve their own lives (and perhaps their children's, present or hoped for), more and more women have been making different choices. The number who have prepared themselves for professional and managerial jobs has skyrocketed in the past two decades (though as Fuchs reminds us, it will take another generation for this change to show up in employment statistics). Women are also returning to work sooner after the birth of children, postponing (or forgoing) having children, and limiting family size.

Fuchs is enthusiastic about women's growing propensity to invest in careers. But he is deeply troubled by two phenomena that he associates with women's efforts to close the economic gender gap: this country's abnormally low birthrate (we have not hit replacement level since 1973) and the rising number of children whose futures are at risk.

Compared with their parents' generation, American children are more likely to commit suicide, perform poorly in school, and show signs of emotional, physical, and mental distress. They are also more likely to live in poverty. In 1960 and 1970, the poverty rate among children was one-third higher than the rate among adults. In 1986, it was almost double (20% versus 11%).

Statistics on the number of children across households and the distribution of income by households can explain the grim poverty figures (although not our willingness as a society to live with those figures). In simple terms, impoverished households are more likely to be headed by a single woman and to include three or more children.

But the reason for the general decline in children's well-being is harder to pin down. Television is one possibility, but Fuchs does not find the evidence compelling. He is more inclined to worry about the decline in parental care and supervision reflected in statistics on the number of hours potentially available to children. On average, children in white households had 10 fewer hours of parental time per week in 1986 than they had in 1960; black children lost 12 hours. The growing number of single parents contributed to this drop, but the chief cause was more working mothers.

For Fuchs, public policy provides a way out of the apparent either-or choice between women's equality and healthy children. Arguing persuasively that all of us have a stake in the next generation's well-being, he proposes child-centered policies that reflect our common social concern, like unrestricted cash grants to mothers of young children. Grants for children would help children directly (a feature that appeals to Fuchs's sense of equity) and would ultimately improve the quality of child care by putting more money in the hands of its purchasers, namely mothers.

But suppose the problem is not financial. Suppose you are one of the fortunate few with access to excellent child care that (almost) never lets you down. That still doesn't deal with the issue of time, the missing parental hours that Fuchs reckons up. I know few working mothers who have not wrestled with this issue and fewer still for whom it is resolved. Yet by and large, I find it troubles fathers a good deal less (if, in fact, it troubles them at all).

One explanation for this discrepancy emerges unexpectedly in the closing pages of Fuchs's book. Commenting on the "fragmentation and fragility" that characterize American family life, he offers advice to potential brides and grooms. "Even in striving for a fifty-fifty marriage," he writes, "it would be wise to be aware of two qualifications. First, it is unlikely that the spouses' contributions can always be equal. . . . Second, 'fifty-fifty' need not mean that each spouse must do half of everything. Specialization need not be gender related, but the partnership gains strength from some division of labor based on innate or acquired skills in particular tasks."

Fuchs's words are evenhanded. He never specifies which spouse should do what. But it is hard to avoid turning his words into pictures—pictures that show mothers and children together at home.

Those images are an appropriate introduction to *The Second Shift*, by Arlie Hochschild, a professor of sociology at the University of California at Berkeley. Over an eight-year period, Hochschild interviewed and observed ten working couples with young children. Struggles over the "second shift"—the phrase comes from one woman who used it to describe the way she felt about the work of taking care of her children and home—are part of every marriage Hochschild observes. But she has very little fifty-fifty accommodation to report. Instead, she shows us family after family in which the wife, willingly or not, consciously or not, does most of the second shift herself—a work load that translates roughly into an extra month of 24-hour days every year. Hochschild explores how the women deal with this, how their husbands feel, and how the strain of the second shift colors their marriages and family lives.

At the same time, Hochschild never loses sight of the many ways in which history and society shape personal choices and private lives (ways I can only touch on here). One of the most valuable aspects of her wise and wide-ranging study is the balance she strikes between individual and communal experience.

Hochschild sees women's movement into paid work as a continuation of the industrial revolution that took men from the farm to the factory. Unlike yesterday's men, however, today's working women have no one to help them ease the transition. There is no longer a "wife" at home to keep the house in order and domestic values alive.

Nor does society take up much slack. When it is six o'clock and getting dinner on the table is one more thing than a working mother can bear, pizza parlors and Chinese restaurants work reasonably well, at least on an occasional basis. But as every working parent knows, we have barely begun to develop good child-care or after-school programs or any of the other social supports that working families badly need. As in every social revolution, people's lives have changed more quickly than institutions—or individual psyches.

Drawing on her observations of the ten couples, as well as on interviews with many other working parents, Hochschild divides men and women into three broad categories on the basis of their attitudes toward home and work. Traditional couples believe that husbands work and women stay home. These beliefs may be a luxury a couple can't afford. (Hochschild found that traditional attitudes were most common among working class couples in which wives worked because they had to.) But at least husband and wife agree where each of them ought to be and how their work should be valued—an agreement that paradoxically makes it easier for the man to go against tradition and help out at home.

Egalitarian couples also agree, but theirs is an equal-commitment model in which husbands and wives spend the same amount of time on their families and careers. Such marriages exist. Hochschild describes two where both husband and wife value the work of child rearing and running a home and share it equitably. But more often, egalitarianism goes along with what Hochschild calls *workaholism à deux*—a common complaint among upper-middle class, professional couples. Life at the office comes first for both partners; life at home is uniformly second-best and relegated to paid help. Children often pay a high price in such families, either because they are largely ignored or because they get too much attention.

Finally, there are transitional couples, a capacious category comprising most of the people Hochschild interviewed and studied. Transitional couples almost always follow a pattern: he does less than she thinks he should. (Though Hochschild has also found marriages in which he is willing to do more but she resists letting him.)

What makes these marriages doubly complicated is that the spouses are often divided inside themselves as well. The images they have of men and women, mothers and fathers, clash with the reality of the lives they lead. What they say they want—a career, to share responsibilities at home—does not mesh with what they feel they ought to do. The computer company vice president who cannot take her own career as seriously as her husband's is a good example. So is the husband who believes he shares the housework because he takes care of the dog—and the wife who finally gave up asking him to do more because she wasn't willing to risk a divorce.

The values and assumptions that lead a couple to this kind of stand-off are deeply rooted in personal history, as Hochschild very carefully makes clear. But as I have said, one of the great strengths of the book is her ability to look at individual lives and choices in context, which is to say, in light of the options society makes available. For the wife in the couple just described, a social worker named Nancy Holt, the only way to keep her identity intact and her marriage going was to see herself as a supermom, that mythic creation who can juggle it all and still smile brightly at the end of the day. What made her fantasy barely plausible was that she could negotiate a part-time arrangement at work.

For women who can't or won't cut back on their jobs, the strain of carrying the second shift rarely lets up. Ironically, two of the executives Hochschild studied worked for a computer company that prided itself on its progressive policies, including flextime, job sharing, and part-time work arrangements. Yet neither of these women felt free to work part time—not because their jobs would not allow it but because their colleagues (male and female) would not countenance it. The message they got was clear: managers showed commitment by working long hours. Needing time with children was no excuse, except that the children did need time, time their fathers could not or would not give.

Eventually, one of these women quit rather than push against the corporate grain, while the other tried working part time, only to be told "I knew you weren't serious" in a hundred different ways. Faced with her bosses' disappointment and the offer of a vice presidency, she decided to return to work full time. But she went with a sinking feeling and with the unspoken proviso that she would quit if her daughter's problems at school got worse.

While quitting might be an option for these particular women (leaving aside, for the moment, the emotional cost), with 70% of American mothers in the work force, it is scarcely a realistic solution across the board. Neither, unfortunately, is the most obvious and easily implemented solution that emerges from Hochschild's book: more paternal involvement in the second shift. As her studies show, most men are remarkably resistant to picking up a meaningful share of the work at home, and looking ahead, she sees more of the same, though perhaps her book will be a catalyst for change. Her conversations with students at Berkeley show that men and women are equally committed to the idea that women should have careers (as does Fuchs's survey of Stanford undergraduates). But taking care of the children and running the house—well, that will be up to mom.

Since Hochschild isn't willing to leave it all to mom, she advocates a host of public policies and initiatives to support working families. These range from workplace interventions, such as tax breaks for companies with family policies, enforcement of comparable worth, and modified hours for parents of small children, to tax-subsidized affordable housing, meal-preparation centers, and traveling day-care vans. Admitting that much of this may sound utopian, she nonetheless reminds us that the eight-hour day, women's suffrage, and the abolition of child labor also sounded utopian not so long ago.

But as *The Second Shift* also reminds us, we live history as we make it. So for every working parent, the questions remain: How do I balance home and work? Can I be a good manager or lawyer or editor and still be a good mom or dad?

In part, of course, the answers to those questions depend as much on our employers as they do on us. If a company's policies make it hard to respond when a child is sick or a day-care arrangement falls apart or a parent conference is scheduled at school, balance will seem and be an impossible goal. But for many parents, the answers also depend on a certain willingness to challenge prevailing norms, among them the assumption that a commitment to being a parent makes you less valuable as an employee.

Felice Schwartz touched on this subject when she mentioned the loyalty that professional and managerial women are likely to feel toward employers that enable them to pursue careers and be mothers. But like many other commentators on this subject, she argues the point in the negative: women can be good managers despite the fact that they have children. I suggest this logic is backward. Women and men can be better managers because they have children.

Consider some of the lessons that being a parent teaches: the importance of consistency, clarity, and structure; the limits to "because I said so" styles of authority; self-discipline and the ability to temper your own wants for the sake of common needs; the benefits of a long-term view, of constancy. Because we know how and where we began to learn these lessons—at home, on the playground—it may seem odd to think of them as management education. But think about dealing with a two-year-old who has just discovered the power of saying "no." The connection will look less far-fetched.

In one sense, parenting is a job like any other. The more time you give it, the better at it you become. (Hochschild reports that fathers who spend more time with their children develop a richer, fuller sense of what it means to be a parent. Experience and observation suggest her insight applies to mothers too.) And that, of course, is where the real conflict arises, since no one can be in two places at once. If we routinely put in 12-hour days at the office, we cannot also spend some of those hours playing with our children or helping them with homework.

But perhaps it is time to rethink the logic that equates long hours with superior performance and workaholism with commitment. In the past dozen years, we have heard a great deal about quality time with children. Within limits, the concept makes sense. (Few working parents need to be told what those limits are. We know the difference between quick time and quality time, and so do our kids.) Maybe now we should apply the concept at work and think less about how many hours we spend in our offices and more about what we do with those hours. At a minimum, it's a question we might each ask ourselves the next time we're about to work late again.

3
The Case of the Part-Time Partner

Gary W. Loveman

Meeker, Needham & Ames, a long-established metropolitan law firm, employs 100 associates and 20 partners and is preeminent in corporate litigation. Each year, the promotions committee nominates associates for promotion. This year, the partner nominations carried particular weight; MN&A's overall billings and partner incomes were stagnating, showing the effects of intensified competition and in-house corporate counsel. The three associates under consideration had all worked for the firm seven years, meeting the minimum requirement for partner.

Chairing the meeting was George Hartwig, 53, for three years the managing partner. Also on the committee were Maury Davidson, 62, a senior partner and managing partner for seven years before Hartwig; Pamela Fisher, 44, a tax law specialist and the only female partner; and Jim Welch, 47, director of litigation.

The day after the meeting, Hartwig circulated the minutes. Memos from Fisher and Davidson appeared on Hartwig's desk the same day.

MEEKER, NEEDHAM & AMES
MINUTES OF THE PROMOTIONS COMMITTEE MEETING
SEPTEMBER 1, 1990
Present: George Hartwig, chair Maury Davidson Pamela Fisher Jim Welch Absent: None

Mr. Hartwig called the meeting to order at noon. He began by reminding the committee that although there was no fixed number of slots available for partners, the committee must consider carefully who it decided to recommend for promotion. Given the severe competition facing the firm, he said, the decision carried with it both risks to the incomes of existing partners and opportunities for new and increased billings. He also stated that the committee should nominate all worthy candidates but should carefully evaluate merit in terms of client service and the ability to generate revenues. He then asked Mr. Davidson to begin the consideration of Rick Stewart.

Mr. Davidson said that he believed that Mr. Stewart should not be promoted to partner. "While Rick has done well at this firm," said Mr. Davidson, "he hasn't really distinguished himself. Nor has he developed a practice that will generate new clients."

Mr. Welch supported Mr. Davidson's position. "Rick's work as a litigator has been solid, as his file indicates. But I don't think he'll become the kind of attorney who can capture the confidence of the high-level executives we want to represent."

Mr. Hartwig asked if anyone wished to support Mr. Stewart. Hearing no one, he declared Mr. Stewart's candidacy dropped and asked Mr. Welch to speak to Tim Brower's candidacy.

Mr. Welch stated that, in his opinion, Mr. Brower could serve as a model for the young, hard-working, committed attorneys the firm would need to attract in the future. "Tim has distinguished himself in virtually every way possible," said Mr. Welch. "He has consistently handled difficult cases with exceptional results and has earned praise from clients. He volunteers for more work and can be found at the office nights and weekends. And he has more than once proposed new legal avenues for us to pursue, based on his expertise in some of the more technical areas of our practice."

Mr. Hartwig asked if there were any reservations to Mr. Brower's candidacy.

Mr. Davidson responded that his only concern was that Mr. Brower seemed more interested in legal technicalities than in pursuing new clients.

Ms. Fisher remarked that his file clearly indicated a lack of new-client development.

Mr. Welch responded that Mr. Brower's networking and client-development abilities were definitely weak but that the rest of his performance was so outstanding that he was certain Mr. Brower could improve in these areas.

Mr. Hartwig asked for the sense of the committee. It unanimously supported Mr. Brower's candidacy for partner.

Mr. Hartwig said that he would introduce the candidacy of Julie Ross. He reminded the committee members that they all had firsthand knowledge of Ms. Ross's capabilities since she had worked for each of them at various times. Her file indicated that they had found her performance exemplary. Her work had ranked among the best in the firm, displaying both keen insight into legal issues and top-notch courtroom litigation. Moreover, Mr. Hartwig stated, in the past two years Ms. Ross had shown a growing capability for attracting new business. In most cases, she had received additional work from existing clients, but in two instances, satisfied clients had given her name to other companies that had then engaged MN&A as their main counsel.

Mr. Hartwig said that the main issue the committee needed to address was Ms. Ross's part-time status. "When Julie had her baby three years ago," he said, "she requested and was given a reduction in her client load. We should consider her promotion in light of how it will affect firm perceptions and policy on part-time status in general."

Mr. Welch asked Mr. Hartwig to review the agreement made with Ms. Ross as well as the firm's other part-time arrangements.

Mr. Hartwig responded that Ms. Ross had negotiated a flexible schedule that permitted her to work "as necessary" to meet the needs of her clients. She and the firm understood that this would require approximately 50% of the billable hours of her colleagues, with salary and benefits reduced accordingly. Mr. Hartwig recalled that there had been much debate about the agreement and that many senior partners had been adamantly opposed to part-time work. Nevertheless, Mr. Hartwig had agreed to the proposal, making MN&A the first firm of its size in the city to implement part-time schedules for its attorneys.

Mr. Hartwig said that after negotiating the agreement with Ms. Ross, he had issued a memorandum stating that the firm would entertain similar requests from other attorneys, would have no general policy on part-time professional work, and would work out decisions and details case by case. Since that time, two other female junior associates had been granted part-time status. Both had negotiated fixed schedules of three days per week.

Ms. Fisher stated that although Ms. Ross exhibited outstanding skills, she was not qualified for promotion. "We all had these skills when we were up for partner. But what distinguished us from the others was our dedication to the firm and to our clients through years of exceptionally hard work and long hours." Ms. Fisher said that as an associate, she had worked a minimum of 70 hours per week, as had most associates who made partner. These long hours were not only evidence of commitment but had also been invaluable in giving her a feel for the firm's distinctive culture and an understanding of its needs. "We have all just agreed that

Mr. Brower should be made partner, in part because of his demonstrated commitment to the firm. Skills alone are not enough," she concluded.

Mr. Welch stated that he agreed with Ms. Fisher that Ms. Ross should not be nominated. "Julie's performance may have been excellent, but it has been based on a less-than-equal standard," Mr. Welch said. He noted that partners had refrained from assigning Ms. Ross the most complex and demanding work because of her limited schedule and her inability to go on lengthy trips. He concluded that he could not support her candidacy unless she returned to work full-time on the same kinds of cases and under the same conditions as her peers.

Ms. Fisher pointed out that the committee needed to address the issue of establishing precedent. "If we promote Julie without demanding an equal commitment to the firm," she stated, "we will be telling all of our associates that we no longer value motivation and dedication."

Mr. Hartwig agreed with Ms. Fisher that Ms. Ross's case would affect the firm's future direction, but he disagreed with her conclusion. He said that the proportion of female law school graduates was increasing each year and with it the number of female associates joining the firm. He pointed out that 40% of new hires in the past five years had been female, yet the firm still had only one female partner. "Our best female associates aren't staying around long enough even to be considered for partner," he stated. "Unless we establish a more flexible environment, we'll continue losing them. Julie is the only promising female candidate we'll have for the next two years. Promoting her will help us attract and retain the best people." Mr. Hartwig concluded that it was in the firm's best interest to balance the costs of nontraditional work schedules against the benefits of keeping people like Ms. Ross.

Mr. Davidson stated that establishing a flexible environment was important to men as well as women. Although no men had yet shifted to part-time schedules, he noted, the firm had recently lost several outstanding male associates who had left to pursue careers that gave them more time with their families. "This is not purely an issue of gender," Mr. Davidson said. "It is an issue of how we structure our work and the demands we place on all of our people. When I came up through the ranks, I expected to work and to do little else. All of us in the partnership paid a very high price in our home and family life, including separation and divorce. Today many of our best associates are unwilling to live as we did, and I can't say I blame them." Mr. Davidson concluded that the firm would have to make some changes in order to keep the best attorneys, and that included promoting Ms. Ross.

Mr. Welch reminded Mr. Hartwig of the debate that had ensued when Ms. Ross was given part-time status as an associate. He predicted that making Ms. Ross a part-time partner would produce an even greater crisis. Mr. Welch said, "I am not convinced that the threat of losing Julie and people like her is worth putting this firm through the convulsions that would follow her promotion. We can always attract enough people like Pam Fisher, Tim Brower, and ourselves among the many associates we hire each year to keep this firm growing and prosperous."

Mr. Hartwig stated that the committee was clearly divided on Ms. Ross's candidacy. Mr. Hartwig said that he would recommend Tim Brower for promotion and would draft a report describing each committee member's arguments regarding Ms. Ross's candidacy. He would circulate the report among the partners and schedule a meeting of the partnership for an open discussion.

Mr. Hartwig adjourned the meeting of the promotions committee at 3:30.

September 2, 1990
To: George Hartwig
From: Pam Fisher

I've just looked over the minutes of the promotions committee meeting, and there are two things I'd like to add.

First, I have to point out, George, that the entire discussion wouldn't have been necessary if, at the time you made the part-time agreement with Julie, you had been explicit about how it would affect her chances of making partner. I don't understand why the issue wasn't clarified from the beginning.

Second, I see an important distinction between part-time associates and part-time partners. I respect Julie's decision to spend time at home with her young child. As an *associate*, I probably would have made the same decision if I'd had children. But I would not have expected to make partner. Associates can cover for other associates, but nobody can cover for a partner; we are the critical link to the client. I need not remind you that this firm is in trouble. I don't think we should consider making someone a partner who would not be working full-time to help us out of this situation.

9/2/90
George—
Nice job handling the discussion at the meeting. You've got a tough

assignment ahead of you outlining for the partners the committee's divergent positions on Julie.

I don't mean to complicate the matter, but to me the issue isn't simply about making Julie a partner. Her case will effectively establish the firm's policy on part-time work. The relevant issues here include flexible work schedules, motivation of both male and female associates, the reaction of the firm's clients, and the concerns of the existing partners.

But even more important, our decision will reflect our beliefs as an organization about how the quality of one's personal life affects one's work at the firm.

I think you know my position on this. I intend to spend more time with my family—I don't want to wait until retirement to begin enjoying my grandkids. Furthermore, I'm convinced that doing this will make the time I spend at the firm more productive.

Maury

Should Meeker, Needham & Ames Make Julie Ross a Partner?

Five experts from both inside and outside the law profession consider this question.

SALLY C. LANDAUER

Meeker, Needham & Ames is a law firm in trouble. It is an associate mill, grinding out young lawyers so rapidly that by the seventh year, only 3 of its 100 associates are left to be considered for partnership.

This should be an economic disaster for the firm. It means that each year it must hire some two to three dozen new associates. Even its second-year associate load must be very heavy. John P. Weil, an Orinda, California law firm consultant, warns that the first-year cost of hiring an associate fresh from law school is $100,000. That includes capital costs, but it also takes into consideration revenue generated. If MN&A hires 30 new associates, it will spend $3,000,000. MN&A cannot afford to lose Julie Ross—despite her part-time status—because she is, by admission of the partnership committee, a client getter.

The committee, however, focused on how Ross's partnership would affect firm perceptions and policies on part-time work in general. The two partners arguing against Ross focused only on her lack of "dedication" to the firm. Pam Fisher, in particular, confuses Ross's part-time schedule with a lack of motivation and dedication. As a mother of three who tried for four years to be a full-time lawyer and an adequate mother, I can assure Fisher that motivation and dedication are not the problem. Despite my present four-day-a-week schedule, I have developed sufficient expertise and enough clients to be asked to join three firms as a partner.

What are the firm's options? Having made the initial mistake of not establishing Julie Ross's position on or off the partnership track at the time she requested part-time status, there are still a number of ways the firm can make Ross a partner. It can:

1. Delay her partnership by an amount of time equivalent to her reduced number of hours. A delay of a year and a half (50% of the three years of part-time work) would enable Ross to reassess whether to stay on a part-time basis at the end of that time or return to full-time work.

2. Establish an income partnership. This option is becoming more common in law firms around the country as competition squeezes profits and as more lawyers reject the 70-hour-a-week work schedule that has traditionally aided partnership entry. With this kind of partnership, Ross would be entitled to partnership status, a guaranteed income rather than points and profit sharing, and the right to vote on all matters except points (compensation) for partners and mergers. She would have no equity investment. She would not share in upside potential, but she would not be exposed to risk, either.

3. Establish a nonequity partnership in which part-time partners participate in profit and loss but make no capital investment and share in none of the firm's assets.

4. Make Ross an equity partner, but establish her level of compensation and investment at 50% of the lowest level of the average compensation of the partners who entered the class ahead of her, her class, and the class behind her. Her points would be determined in the same manner. She would always be compensated less than others similarly situated, but that is the price she must pay for the privilege of part-time status.

5. Make her a nonequity partner for five years, with a move up to equity after that time.

One final note. A litigation-only firm will have more difficulty with part-time associates and part-time partners than a business or transactional firm; court appearances, depositions, and trials frequently cannot be arranged around a part-time schedule. A transactional attorney, on the other hand, can often arrange his or her practice around the part-time schedule.

To be competitive in today's recruiting marketplace, MN&A must change its policies. It is throwing years of investment down the hole if it rejects Julie Ross as a partner. She will have no choice but to seek employment elsewhere, taking her considerable skills and her obviously growing practice with her. MN&A cannot afford to lose Julie Ross or to set a precedent that part-time is a career dead end.

MARSHA E. SIMMS

My gut reaction as a woman was that of course Julie Ross should become a partner at MN&A. But when I considered the issue in light of the realities of today's law firms and businesses, I concluded that she should not. A partner in any professional firm has to have made a conscious decision to have a career. Julie Ross has decided she wants a job—not a career.

Part-time partnership raises important issues for clients, peers (male and female), and other women in the firm.

The firm's clients. While there will be some clients who can work within a part-time partner's time constraints, most clients expect a partner to be available whenever needed. A partner also has to be willing to work to expand the client base and to work with any client of the firm who needs that person's expertise. Julie Ross wants to limit her practice to meeting the needs of only her clients (so long as those needs are not full-time), not the firm's.

The part-time partner's peers. Without a doubt, making someone a partner who has not "suffered" as much as his or her peers creates resentment in the partnership. While most lawyers have reached a point where they accept "stopping out" for a limited period for whatever reason (maternity leave or a sabbatical, for instance), they expect their partners to be the people who have made and are willing to continue to make the same commitment as they have to the firm over an extended period. If someone is not willing to make that commitment, then peers will question whether that person should be given a status that symbolizes the commitment.

Other women in the firm. Most women who have attained a level of professional success have done so by consciously sacrificing other aspects of their lives—whether it be marriage, children, or community involvement. They have discovered that they can't have it all and have had to choose what they want most. Creating a new set of partnership criteria for part-time associates, most of whom will be women, risks alienating women who have earned their status in the traditional way and have made the sacrifices Julie Ross was unwilling to make. Such a policy might also imply that women should be judged by a different, less demanding set of criteria, which brings into question the competency and commitment of all professional women.

I am not suggesting, however, that MN&A reject for all time the possibility of making Julie Ross a partner. If she ever returns to work full-time, then she should be considered for partnership. If at that time she is still performing at the same level that she is now, she should be made a partner.

MN&A could have avoided its dilemma by discussing with Julie Ross (and then making it a part of its announced policy) at what point, if any, an associate who works part-time would be considered for partnership. Unfortunately, most firms have no policy on part-time employment or other nontraditional work roles and instead treat each case on an ad hoc basis. This approach makes it difficult for those who are contemplating a part-time arrangement to evaluate how it might affect their futures. Also, the resulting disparate treatment of different part-time requests creates its own set of problems.

The most workable policy in a law firm, therefore, is one in which associates are permitted to take leaves of absence or work part-time schedules with the understanding that they will have to return to work full-time before they can be considered for partnership. For those who do not want to be considered for partnership, the firm should try to work out a mutually satisfactory schedule. As one MN&A partner mentioned, the firm cannot afford to lose intelligent lawyers because of its unwillingness to be flexible.

WALTER R. TROSIN

This case raises an important question: Given that most employees who are parents have a spouse who also works, how can companies address the needs of employees who have dual obligations?

In Julie Ross's case, MN&A could not begin to answer this question because it did not think through the implications of her part-time arrangement at the time it was made. George Hartwig should have, for instance, asked Ross what kinds of expectations she had from the firm and whether she would be willing to make child-care arrangements when emergencies arose at work. And he should have let her know the extent of the firm's commitment to her and what chance she had for partnership.

At this point, the firm can at least revisit the terms of the agreement it made with Ross. For instance, did a part-time schedule mean she would be working 25 hours a week or 40? This will also force the firm to examine its requirements for partner. Given the reality of pressures from an increasingly stressful world outside the office, including but not limited to family obligations, is MN&A (and other businesses) really benefiting from a tradition of working its employees 70 hours a week?

Within MN&A's present culture of "hit the ground running and keep your nose to the grindstone," I would be very reluctant to make Ross a full-time partner. In such a firm, it would send a signal that hard work is not necessary to move forward. Still, MN&A should discuss with Ross the possibility of granting her a limited partnership status or allowing her to share her partnership with another person who has a similar arrangement.

At Merck, we base promotion decisions on how well individuals perform and on our judgment of their ability to perform at a higher level. We expect people to work hard and to be dedicated—but we do not expect them to give up their families. In fact, I believe (as Maury Davidson implies in his memo) that workers are most effective when they do *not* work constantly.

As is the case with a growing number of companies, Merck has part-time work policies—and we have found that they have unexpected payoffs: for example, part-time employees frequently focus more on task completion and getting jobs done rather than simply on attendance. And doing the job, after all, is what we pay employees for.

Nevertheless, it is only nonmanagers that work part-time at Merck; we don't have managerial part-time work. It would be very difficult for a senior manager to work part-time because, let's face it, supervising is a full-time job. The only possible way managers could work part-time is on a job-sharing basis. The rules here are still emerging; Merck, for instance, has not yet dealt with this. Given the increasing need in our diverse work force for more flexible approaches, however, we may have to address this sooner rather than later.

BARBARA MENDEL MAYDEN

Let me get this straight. Julie Ross has displayed exemplary performance as a lawyer, and unlike her colleague Tim Brower who is being nominated for promotion, she has demonstrated revenue-generation skills. She passes the tests articulated by the firm.

Why should the number of hours Ross works, an arrangement approved by the firm, determine whether she should be made a partner? Is it some sort of initiation rite? While a firm may decide that the attributes it is looking for in a partner may take longer to attain working part-time, when those criteria are met, what does a threshold number of hours add to that equation?

Experience, expertise, and other effects of tenure that Ross gained while working an alternative schedule should not fall into a black hole. She is a lawyer who has attained skills, has garnered firm and client respect, and has presumably done her *pro rata* share of *pro bono*, community service, and firm administration. She should accordingly be promoted.

Yet Pam Fisher argues that because she and her colleagues worked 70-hour weeks, so should anyone who comes up behind them. Fisher's memory may be a little clouded by fatigue; legal management firms tell us that the billable-hour spiral is much higher than this. In the late 1970s, average annual billables for associates hovered around 1,700 hours, which today would be considered "part-time" compared with the more than 2,000 billable hours associates now average.

So should Ross, who bills, say, 1,500 hours a year working part-time, take home the same amount of money as Brower, who bills 3,000 hours? Of course not. (After all, the 3,000-hour-a-year lawyer will likely have alimony and child support to pay.) Hours worked may be relevant to the size of Ross's piece of the pie but not to her ability to sit down at the table.

Jim Welch believes that the firm needs a young, hard-working, committed attorney for a model. But maybe the focus of that model ought instead to be talent, efficiency, and values. Reporter Marilyn Goldstein, in an article appearing last year in *New York Newsday*, wrote:

> The question should not be what's wrong with a woman who doesn't want to work 12-hour days but what's wrong with a man who does—and a culture that . . . applauds, glorifies, promotes people who put their jobs before their families . . . This penchant for promotions via . . . overtime reflects an assumption that those will-

ing to work long hours are the best and brightest (but) maybe the ones willing to work long hours are just the ones willing to work long hours. . . . What if we discover the answer to moving American commerce and industry ahead is finding those smart enough *not* to work 12-hour days and turning the reins of business over to them? Who knows, we might come up with a mother lode of talent.

Implicit in the discussion about whether to make Ross a partner is that it is uneconomic to do so. Some of the most successful law firms in the country, however, have shown that alternative work schedules that don't "mommy track" women into pink-collar, no-room-for-advancement ghettos can be profitable. Those firms report that their reduced-schedule lawyers—both partners and associates—demonstrate increased productivity with a higher ratio of billable hours to hours worked. Fixed costs relating to such lawyers can be reduced. Fears about part-time partners being unable to supervise or to deal with client concerns have not been borne out; more often than not, the partner on an alternative work schedule is more accessible than the 2,500-hour-a-year workaholic juggling too many matters.

Firms that don't provide a work environment where family and professional responsibilities can be reconciled will lose their most valuable resources—many of their best people—to firms that are more "family friendly." Retention of valued, experienced professionals produces distinct value. Firm costs escalate with lawyer turnover. When firms don't offer options, they lose lawyers just when they have become profitable. (It has been noted that a woman professional's most productive years are also her reproductive years.) Clients become frustrated finding their matters constantly being shifted to new lawyers unfamiliar with their circumstances.

How firms deal with balancing family and work responsibilities is not just a women's issue, as Maury Davidson points out in the case. Perhaps women were the first to notice these issues, but what is becoming increasingly evident is that men are now leaving firms in greater numbers. No longer is the prototypical new lawyer a man who was put through school by a working wife who remains at home after her husband becomes a lawyer and devotes herself to providing her husband and children with a well-organized home life. Today both women and men are dealing with more responsibilities at home, in addition to those at the office. Men are increasingly opting out of those firms that cultivate an obvious "bottom-line only" environment. The managing partner of a major New York law firm recently noted that even men who don't intend to work part-time or take parental leave look for these kinds of policies in firms because they reveal how much importance a firm places on family issues.

Jim Welch is naive to think that without flexible policies, MN&A will continue to attract young lawyers of the quality of Fisher and Brower. While the lure of the big money was once all-powerful, law students are now becoming aware of the downside of a law firm environment where a 2,500-hour-billable-year expectation is not uncommon. In evaluating law firms, they are looking beyond the highest bidder and at the importance of lifestyle and family issues.

Pam Fisher is concerned about the message the firm will send by making Julie Ross a partner. With proper guidance from the top (and a written policy clearly articulating the firm's reasoning and the parameters of the policy), the other associates and potential recruits will see that Ross is a hard-working lawyer who has excelled in her field and who has traded the extra hours demanded of others for a significant cut in pay and benefits. And they will see MN&A as an organization that has responded to the demographics of the 1990s and that understands the importance of maintaining human values in a busy, successful legal practice.

D. TIMOTHY HALL

It is crucial at this point in MN&A's history that it take innovative action: it should promote Julie Ross.

First, let's look at the state of affairs for law firms and businesses alike. The emergence of global marketing and technological innovations means that our world has never been more competitive. And the most competitive assets for any business, as the saying goes, leave the building each night (however late the departure might be!). The only way to grow a business in these uncertain times is through a clear strategy of recruiting and grooming the finest talent available.

MN&A's three central criteria in evaluating partner candidates are: (1) legal performance, (2) commitment to the firm's work, and (3) client service and ability to generate new business. There is no doubt that Ross's performance is outstanding on the first and third criteria. But she has also been outstanding in the second area—when measured against the expected commitment level the firm negotiated with her. Furthermore, based on what George Hartwig says, Ross is the kind of lawyer who is committed to do whatever it takes to serve a given client, regardless of the number of hours a week she has agreed to work.

MN&A has to redefine the word "commitment" to mean whatever it takes to meet client needs—not a particular number of hours spent at the office each week. It must then let everyone at the firm know that this new commitment to *service* (rather than *hours*) will be its major strategic advantage. In effect, this will create a new psychological contract between the firm and its staff: if an employee performs well, shows commitment and flexibility, and opens up new areas of business, the firm will provide financial rewards, professional growth opportunities, a long-term relationship, and flexible work options.

For MN&A's current partners, this means new rules. MN&A acknowledged that the rules had changed when it implemented flexible work for associates. The rules have had to change because the game has changed: employees in all business realms are needing and insisting on more flexibility.

The most important thing is to make changes discussable. MN&A employees need information about what to expect under the new contract. For example, employees working part-time may need to modify their career goals and expect to be promoted more slowly than their full-time counterparts.

As part of this communication process, MN&A will also need to give suitable recognition to its current partners who made family trade-offs so they could serve the firm full-time. George Hartwig needs to let people like Pam Fisher and Tim Brower know how much he values their contributions and that he realizes that they had fewer options. As MN&A communicates its new career contract more widely, inside and outside the firm, not only will it retain and develop key assets like Julie Ross but it will also be better able to attract other women and men of her caliber who want a work-family balance that other firms aren't yet offering.

This kind of new contract is an opportunity for a business to create a strategic human-resource-development plan. This would entail examining future needs for skills and experience, the extent to which those needs are already being met, what gaps exist, and a plan for addressing those gaps by recruiting, selecting, developing, retaining, and rewarding future staff.

A staff task force could be appointed to work on this plan. It could survey clients to assess their future needs, and it could survey staff at all levels to assess career and personal needs. The task force could then develop an overall plan with policy recommendations addressing issues like flexible work arrangements, career timetables, compensation and benefit policies, career coaching and mentoring, and dependent care. The plan could be communicated and discussed with all staff in a variety of settings—regular staff meetings, a company newsletter, partner meetings, or "brown bag" lunch seminars.

Included in such a plan could be a lengthened timetable for part-timers. If a major objection to Ross's candidacy is that she has not yet done the same volume of work as her full-time peers, MN&A might require her to work additional years until she has.

Similarly, it might establish different levels of partnership to deal with the compensation issue and the concern that part-time partners might bring in less new business. One level would be fully participating partners who would share in the profits of the firm. A second level would be salaried partners who would not share in firm profits. Salaried partners could be either part-timers or technical specialists who would not generate business; in addition to lower financial return, they would have the advantage of lower risk since they would not sign firm loans or otherwise participate in the firm's investments. A few Boston law firms have already adopted this structure, and public accounting firms have implemented comparable structures.

Another option might be to allow employees to move from one level to another as their circumstances change. In addition to keeping the full-partner role open for part-timers, this could also be a way for older, fully participating partners to phase gradually into retirement or to continue working longer than they otherwise would—without the pressures of full-profit participation and contribution.

Regardless of what the new plan includes, the key is to make it discussable. This should be easy in a firm the size of MN&A. George Hartwig should act quickly to meet the needs of both the staff and the firm and use this opportunity to gain a strategic advantage over competitors.

Note

At the time of this article's publication Sally C. Landauer was a partner at Ball, Janik & Novack, a Portland, Oregon law firm. Marsha E. Simms was a partner at Weil, Gotshal & Manges, a New York City law firm. Walter R. Trosin was vice president of strategy and development for Merck & Co., Inc. Barbara Mendel Mayden practiced law in New York City and was a member of the American Bar Association Commission on Women in the Profession. D. Timothy Hall was a professor of organizational behavior and associate dean for faculty development in the school of management at Boston University.

PART
IV
Tales from the Front

1

From the Classroom to the Corner Office

Rosemarie B. Greco

I am CEO of a $5.7-billion bank. My career in banking is the unexpected outcome of an aspiration I had as a six-year-old, when I told anyone who would listen that I wanted to be a teacher. I was the youngest of six children from a working-class neighborhood in South Philadelphia, and my dream of being a teacher was neither extraordinary nor uncommon. In fact, it was a dream voiced by many girls of my era.

I didn't know then how lucky I was to choose one of the few professions open to women at that time. And I certainly didn't know that teaching and managing are much the same profession. All I knew was that I admired my own teachers and that I was determined to do everything to the best of my ability. The rest came to me gradually—first at a convent, then at a bank—as I learned two essential lessons: that both women and men can shape their own professional destinies and that there is unlimited power in the fusion of organizational vision and individual fulfillment.

Now every day I help people grow to their fullest potential, and I help move the corporation toward its own goals. I set standards, communicate values, and impart knowledge—all things that a good teacher must do well. Indeed, throughout my 24-year career in banking, I have always considered myself a teacher first and a banker second.

When I was in the sixth grade, I told my father I was going to be the first child from our family to go to college, and there was no doubt in my mind that I would use my degree to teach. But life changed irrevocably when my dad died suddenly of a heart attack in 1962. I was 16 years old and forced to face many realities, including one that I had long ignored. We were poor. My father had always called me his princess, but we were far from royalty. Learning quickly that I would soon have to take a job to help support my family, I transferred out of the college preparatory program at school and into the secretarial program, where I took shorthand and typing.

In my senior year of high school, I went to my prom in a $10 gown my mother rented for me. I proudly wore my only piece of jewelry, the class ring that my brother and sisters had chipped in to buy. A few weeks before graduation, I took the government's clerk-typist exam and passed. I could have gone into the civil service, but there was also a program in the Archdiocese of Philadelphia that allowed honors graduates to teach in parochial schools while attending college part-time. The government paid $60 a week, the Catholic schools $37 a week.

I went home and explained my dilemma to my mother and other members of the family. She said, "You've always wanted to be a teacher, I know that's your dream, and I want you to be educated, so go and teach." That's how I started teaching third grade at Our Lady of Mt. Carmel in the heart of South Philadelphia. I was 17 years old, and I had 67 students.

In the fervor of the 1960s, all dreams were passionate, and mine was no exception. If I was going to be a teacher, I believed teaching should be my life's work. So, at 19, I joined the Convent of the Sister Servants of the Immaculate Heart of Mary at Immaculata College in Immaculata, Pennsylvania. It was and is one of the most accomplished teaching orders in the country.

I expected to learn the science of teaching; what I actually learned was the art of management. As novices, we each had specific job responsibilities. My assignment was to be the valet, secretary, and driver for the Mother General of the Religious Order, a title and function not unlike CEO and chairman of a major corporation. Mother General Maria Pachis was an exceptional leader and a visionary— warm, outgoing, inspirational, smart, and tough. During the time that I was in the convent, she oversaw a major construction project: the building of a House of Studies for novices, analogous to a corporate training center complete with lodging facilities for 300 permanent residents.

I was at Sister Pachis's side as she talked to every single person involved in the project, her habit trailing in the dirt at those dusty construction sites. She knew the first names of the bricklayers, the construction company owner, and the bankers who financed the project. Sister Pachis couldn't learn to lay bricks the way I would later learn to be a bank teller, but she understood the whole process, and she made her presence felt at every level.

I didn't know it at the time, but walking beside her, scribbling notes furiously, I experienced the connections between teaching and managing that would serve me so well later in my career. Sister Pachis managed the construction process the way she taught in the classroom. She helped analyze a problem and devise alternative solutions, then led the process to a conclusion. She encouraged people to participate, but she always made the tough decisions. Everyone owned the victory, but underneath it all, no one doubted who had led the charge.

Over the next three years, working with Sister Pachis, teaching first grade, and completing full semesters of college credit bolstered my self-esteem. Although my superiors tried hard to teach me humility, my self-confidence grew daily. Beyond the walls of the convent, I saw a whole new world evolving for women, and some of the same reasons that brought me inside the convent gates propelled me outside once again.

Back home, I found there was even less money in the house than when I'd left three years before. My mother was 62 and still working 10 hours a day as a cook. Family finances were stretched so thin that she'd been forced to sell my piano, my most prized possession and the last gift I had received from my father. She had also given away all my clothes. One of my sisters was about my size, so I had a few of her dresses altered to fit me. I went out to look for work in hand-me-down clothing.

In the late 1960s, the exodus of people from religious life had just begun, and employers were not comfortable with former nuns. My job applications were rejected time and time again. One interviewer actually said to me, "I really don't think you'd like working here because you might hear four-letter words." I reminded him that I had been born and raised in South Philadelphia, where I'd heard those words many times before—in both Italian and English.

A month to the day after I left the convent, I was hired by Fidelity Bank as a secretary at a branch scheduled to open in midsummer of 1968. I started working there in the spring, so I had plenty of time to learn about the different services the bank offered. Every day I asked someone to teach me something new—how a corporation was formed, when a client should consider a trust, or how to open accounts. And in a special three-ring binder, I took careful notes. At night, I brought home blank forms and agreements and described the process for completing them in my notebook.

By the time the branch opened, my three-ring binder was almost three inches thick. It was my personal guidebook and soon became the bank's first official training manual. At that time, the bank was hiring many military officers just back from Vietnam as branch managers. There was no formal training program to prepare them for their new jobs, so I volunteered to teach them using my book. Many people have asked me since, "Didn't you think that was terrible? There you were, just a branch secretary, training men who were going to be managers and make twice as much as you?" But that thought never entered my mind. I was teaching and helping people, and I was making money—money I needed to go back to school. I thought I was getting the best of all possible worlds.

By the following June, I had saved enough to buy a few necessary personal items, like a new winter coat. I still needed to work, but I wanted to teach. When I was offered a job at a school in the suburbs, I tried to resign the next day. But my branch manager said to me, "You can't quit! The regional vice president wants you to be his secretary and help train people in his area." He offered me a big raise: something like ten dollars more a week. It wasn't much, but it added up to a lot more than I would have made teaching. And the bank had a tuition reimbursement program so I could keep working toward my degree in education.

Two years and two job promotions later, I was transferred to human resources to be part of the bank's new centralized training function. I put together a three-page memo on training programs, which I thought the bank sorely needed, for my new boss. He never acknowledged my ideas, and I assumed he hadn't found them worthwhile. Then, to my great surprise, some of my programs were introduced at the very top of our organization. I couldn't understand why no one had consulted me or given me any credit. Eventually I discovered that my boss had used correction fluid to remove my name from the proposals and replaced it with his own. When I asked him why he had done such a thing, he replied, "Well, I knew you would want what was best for the bank, and your ideas would never have been implemented coming from so far down the ladder."

I jumped from confusion to shock to real anger. I'd always thought if you worked hard and excelled, you would be rewarded for your work. I believed that in the business world, everything was a perfect meritocracy. But, of course, no organization is really that way. Suddenly I found myself on an uneven playing field, facing two equally tough choices. I could stay and fight, or I could leave. And I knew that even if I went to battle, I couldn't win. My boss had the support of our superiors, and at the time it wasn't a corporate culture that touted fairness as one of its values. I decided to exit the playing field but not the arena. I sold the concept of specialized training to the operations department.

In those days, operations was a less than sophisticated back-room function in which thousands of checks were processed each day. There was nothing prestigious about being an operations employee, and more than a few people told me I was making a mistake that bordered on professional suicide. But there, at least, I assumed the playing field was flat.

I was 28 when I went to the operations department as its training director. At the same time, I graduated magna cum laude from Saint Joseph's University, where I had been attending night school. I thought surely I had arrived and expected to wrap my new sheepskin around my first five-figure salary. I considered earning $10,000 a year to be a real watershed for me, a true mark of distinction as a professional.

Well, the head of operations didn't think I was worth $10,000 a year, and he said so. In my entire career, I've only been moved to tears twice. Walking out of the executive vice president's office that day, I retreated to a stairwell and cried. It seemed at the time that I would never get any bank officer to value my education or professional contribution. Returning to my desk, I reviewed my options. It was January, and I could hardly find a teaching job in the middle of the school year. I decided to do the only thing possible: prove to my new boss that I was worth $10,000 a year. The operations department had a critical human resources problem.

The clerks who were hired to process checks, which in those days included stuffing statements into mailing envelopes, were young women fresh out of high school. If statement stuffing fell on a Friday night, many of these 18-year-olds opted for parties over employment. Turnover in operations was off the charts and the amount of time spent training new hires inordinately high.

Though I had no direct influence over operational processes at the time, I could reduce training hours. I created instruction booklets that taught, tested, and retaught the basic steps in check processing. In order to write the text for these booklets, I worked day and night shifts, learning firsthand how to do a dozen or so critical jobs like bookkeeper, proof-machine operator, and stop-payment clerk. And in the process, I discovered that neither employees nor supervisors understood the importance of their work or how it all fit into the journey of a check—from the moment it was written until it was returned in the customer's statement. So I set out to explain it to them.

The public relations department had just bought the bank's first video camera. In exchange for teaching an aspiring public relations executive assistant how to write form letters, the camera was released into my "safekeeping." While another colleague worked the camera, I walked through every operating unit, explaining how one group's work contributed to another's. We had no editing capabilities at the bank, so I had to teach for an hour at a time without making any mistakes. My hours of practice before taping forced me to reflect on the interdependence of the operating units—how their collective success in meeting deadlines and maintaining quality standards was tied to the total process.

The training booklets and my video resulted in a significant decline in turnover in operations and many improvements in check-processing efficiency. Four months after my tearful stairwell experience, the executive vice president summoned me into his office. "You were right," he said, handing me a payroll form. That's all he said—"You were right"—but it was enough. Finally I had become a five-figure professional.

Two years later, in the early 1970s, the bank faced a sex discrimination class-action suit filed by a computer programmer. She had worked for Fidelity as a part-time teller during her summer breaks from college and joined us full-time as a programmer after her graduation. One of the first projects she worked on gave her access to the bank's entire payroll. In sorting through files, this programmer discovered that a man who did the same job and had the same level of education and computing experience was making several thousand dollars a year more than she was. The angry programmer made an appointment with the only senior woman in human resources to object to such an inequity in pay. She was told that her male coworker had a wife and children to support; in other words, he was entitled to more money for the same job.

After a long and arduous legal battle, the bank signed a court-ordered consent decree promising never again to do what we had never admitted to doing in the first place—discriminate against women. There were no hiring or promotion quotas in the agreement, only a requirement that the bank create a job-grading and posting system for all professional openings and ensure that women and minorities were included in the applicant pool. Senior managers at the bank believed human resources staff members were writing the necessary job descriptions. But two weeks before the bank was due to file its final plan for court approval, they learned that the project was nowhere near completion.

The president appointed six of us to complete the project. Working around the clock for two weeks straight, we wrote several hundred job descriptions and then created a job-grading system. Our first stop was Philadelphia's Mercantile Library, where we collected the few articles and one book available on the subject of salary-grading systems. Given the scarcity of resources and time, I read aloud to the team from our borrowed material as we worked in near silence, a practice reminiscent of the silent meditative convent moments of my past.

Understanding job-grading systems was a welcome and unexpected consequence of this project. But slotting employees into the newly created job grades led me to discover a truth about my company's corporate culture that I'd avoided in the past. Even in the same or similar jobs, the work of men was valued much more highly than that of women. Suddenly I realized that in teaching "men only" to be branch managers when I was a secretary and in failing to translate my former boss's comment of "from so far down the ladder" to "because the ideas came from a woman" I had been an unwitting accomplice in perpetuating Fidelity's corporate culture. But that was about to change.

When the work of the panel was over, the president assigned me to a temporary stint in human resources. In my new position, I ran the division and implemented the new job-posting system. He also hired a new vice president of human resources—a woman who had a Ph.D., had worked as a national consultant on affirmative action programs, and was a self-proclaimed feminist.

It soon became painfully clear that this woman would not succeed. Since she thought of herself as a woman who was entitled to the job rather than a manager who must do the job, she became an easy target for male colleagues who wanted to undermine her.

Within a relatively short period of time, she left Fidelity, and I was asked to head human resources. My new responsibilities included the management of all training and development for the bank. My former boss was now one of my direct reports, and I soon saw that he hadn't corrected his "white-out ways." His staff was a demoralized and fearful group. And so, as my first official and symbolic act, determined as I was to right Fidelity's discriminatory culture, I fired him.

That particular action met with a round of applause, which reverberated throughout the bank. It was one of my more popular moves. Over the years, lots of people have also applauded after hearing this story. They certainly thought my action was justified. But I didn't fire him out of simple retribution or revenge. I've always tried to do what was right for the bank—not what felt best for me as a person or what would advance my career.

I quickly forced other necessary actions, policies, and procedures that weren't so popular. When Fidelity had to make layoffs, I met with the managers and asked them to design a plan to rank their employees according to their performance. Not surprisingly, women were often ranked at the bottom in this process. I challenged many of these rankings because I knew how to do many of those jobs myself and had trained a number of the employees who had been relegated to the bottom of their supervisors' lists. Department heads accused me of infringing on their prerogative as managers—and I was indeed guilty of the offense.

While these managers had appreciated my intervention and solutions as the operations training director, they resisted and resented my plans to change the corporate culture as head of human resources. Often the only reassurance I had was my recollection of something a master teacher had once whispered in my ear at the end of a particularly trying classroom period. "They don't have to like what you say," she had said, "they only have to learn from what you do."

Sometimes teachers have to be unpopular. They have to force their students to learn things that are unpleasant or in direct opposition to what people would like to believe. The same is true for managers. We can't only teach the technical side of our business; often we must be in the uncomfortable position of teaching, changing, or reinforcing values in our corporation. We must have an unwavering commitment to doing the right thing—and the ability to grow a second layer of tough skin.

Nearly a decade after the consent decree was signed, Fidelity Bank was featured as one of 50 organizations in Baila Zeitz and Lorraine Dusky's book *The Best Companies for Women* (Simon and Schuster, 1988).

In 1978, a major management upheaval occurred at the bank, including a changing of the guard at the most senior level. The new CEO was a dynamic and innovative leader. Among the most surprising changes he made was appointing me as head of branch banking, then adding the responsibility for Fidelity's small business banking a year later. These were both high-profile lines of business with less than stellar track records. I reminded our new CEO that I hadn't worked in the branches since my secretarial days, had never been a branch manager, and obviously had never made a commercial loan in my life. His unforgettable response was "You can learn the business. I need you to teach the people how to change."

At the time, a local accounting firm had taken a survey to see how small businesses rated their banks. In the ranking of eight banks in the area, Fidelity was near last or dead last in every relevant category. My goal was to develop and implement a plan that would place us at the very top of the next survey. Working with skilled lenders and strategic planners, I analyzed the problem, sought counsel from external experts—our small business customers—and went to class with our commercial lender trainees to learn the basics.

Within a matter of weeks, a small group of believers and I started implementing a plan that would move the lending officers from their comfortable offices at headquarters to nine new locations throughout five counties, placing them closer to our customers. We defined prospect goals, an account call-reporting system, and performance standards in terms of customer response time—and introduced an incentive program as reinforcement. It wasn't the biggest reward package imaginable, but it was better than a turkey and a bottle of Cold Duck at Christmas.

A number of the lending officers did not support the plan. When I announced the changes I wanted made, there were people in that room whose lives were going to change dramatically, and they were angry. Later, after several one-on-one interviews with each staffperson, I determined who believed in the new vision, who would never see it as the right thing to do, and who could be taught. For those who could not or would not, there was a generous severance package.

One of the earliest lessons I ever learned about affecting corporate culture came during my convent days. The nuns totally embraced the precepts of the Church. They understood its mission clearly, and as individuals, they determined their measure by a set of standards inextricably tied to a common goal. The internal culture and customer perception of small business banking could never have changed without everyone involved embracing a common vision, understanding the rationale of our mission, and behaving as a community of people in pursuit of the same goal. And in a follow-up survey conducted three years later by the same accounting firm, our bank was ranked first or second in all of the categories that mattered.

I think there's a moment in everyone's life when they come to the realization that every work experience they've ever had has shaped who they are as much as what they are.

My moment of truth came on a December morning in 1988, when I summoned our bank officers to the cafeteria to deliver some devastating news. By then, I'd been president of the bank for nearly two years, and we were in the throes of a tumultuous "merger of equals" between our corporation and First Fidelity Bancorporation of New Jersey. The Philadelphia bank was the first major commercial bank in the country to declare significant real-estate loan problems at the end of the 1980s. The impact of the losses was compounded by a power struggle at the parent corporation, and in reality our "merger of equals" meant that our bank had been acquired.

In a board meeting the night before, our CEO and vice chairman had been forced to resign. These men were greatly admired, and I knew my colleagues would feel a shock equal to my own. When I approached the cafeteria doors, I was struck by the eerie silence inside the room. Eight hundred voices had been muted by sadness and anxiety.

As I stood on the makeshift platform, I looked into the faces of people I had trained while in operations, hired when in human resources, made countless decisions with, learned many lessons from, and constructed a new corporate culture with. Many of them were in tears. I saw that these officers needed to be comforted, encouraged, and, most of all, led. I promised them we would get through these difficult times together. I assured them that our bank was safe and sound and gave them a critical assignment—to convince our customers that they had made the right choice in banking with us.

For months after this meeting, I met with people from 6:30 in the morning until 9:30 at night, repeating and reinforcing the touchstones of our corporate culture: service to the customer and respect for each other. In the end, our employees came through once again.

In September 1990, under a new corporate administration, I was elected chief executive officer of the Philadelphia bank and a senior executive vice president of the corporation. On that day, I was again standing on a makeshift stage while balloons bounced in the air and a tape played "Hail to the Chief." Many of the hundreds of faces were those of colleagues I had known for half my life and through the dozens of jobs I'd held in my 22 years at Fidelity Bank.

I told them that my new title had really been earned for me by them. It was a vindication of our bank and a testimony to their individual and collective strength. And as I stepped off the stage, something inside also told me that all the lessons I could teach there had been taught.

Six months later, I left Fidelity for good. But I didn't go far. I became president and chief executive officer of the rival bank across town— CoreStates First Pennsylvania Bank. The first thing I did was buy a notebook. And I began again.

2
The Purpose at the Heart of Management

Kye Anderson

I am the chairman, CEO, and president of a profitable, rapidly growing medical technology company that I founded on my dining room table. Single-mindedly, I invented a technology, sold my ideas to doctors and investors, and built a corporation with 130 employees and $15 million in sales. The drive to invent, found, sell, and build came from inside, from one of those legendary entrepreneurial wellsprings of zeal and inspiration. But where entrepreneurs are well equipped with passion, we are also notoriously bad managers. I hated delegating authority, for example, and I was not a good planner—or even a good communicator when it came to my employees. The ability and willingness to delegate, communicate, plan, and preach the vision—most of the skills it took to lead the company past the magic $10 million mark in sales—were capacities I had to acquire.

Companies as well as people have to grow up. In business, the name for this maturity is management. And yet that's only a half truth. To succeed, startup enterprises need both passion *and* good management. If youthful fire and intensity are not enough to build a successful company, technique alone is no better. Pushing a new enterprise past all the barriers to success takes learnable skills to be sure, but it also takes a tenacious inner passion bordering on monomania. This combination is what I call leadership.

When I was 13 years old, my father had a massive heart attack. He was 47 years old, an active man, a former athlete, but he was sometimes so short of breath that he would rush out of the house in a panic, thinking he'd be able to breathe better in the open air. He even went to the hospital, but the doctors could find nothing wrong with him; his electrocardiogram was normal. All they could say was, "Well, it's not your heart."

But it was his heart. Two weeks after his ECG, he had what was probably a myocardial infarction. When I heard, I left school and ran all the way to the hospital—a mile or so in the little town where we lived. Because I was so young, they wouldn't let me in, so I ran around the building looking in windows until I spotted my mother. I got her to come to the front desk and take me to Dad's room.

He wasn't dead, but he was in an oxygen tent with needles in his arms, and his face was blue. I stayed at the hospital all day, while my mother sat beside the bed and held Dad's hand. Every now and then a nurse would come in and check the tubes, and once a doctor came in and studied the ECG made earlier that day.

I sat up on top of the radiator cover and kept thinking two thoughts over and over again. The first was a prayer: "He's so sick, dear God, please help him."

The second had to do with the electrocardiograph. It was pretty high tech for Crosby, Minnesota in 1959, but I was so scared for my father, I simply wasn't impressed. I just kept staring at the tape that came out of it and thinking, "Is that all they know? He's so sick, and all they know is that squiggly line?"

I remember asking my mother what was wrong with him and her saying, "They don't know."

I understand now that they couldn't have known. There was almost no way for them to tell. Diagnostics was more an art than a science in those days because doctors had so little objective information to work with.

Worse yet for Dad and thousands of others, they had no way of detecting heart disease early enough to prevent a heart attack. The electrocardiograph was virtually their only diagnostic weapon, and what an ECG reveals is damage to the heart muscle. It can't detect a developing problem in time to head it off, it can only show anatomical changes as and after they occur. Probably, Dad's heart had been dying slowly for weeks. That was why he'd been so short of breath—his heart wasn't pumping enough blood to supply his body with oxygen. But 1950s diagnostics couldn't pinpoint the problem until after the harm was done. In the end, his heart was so diseased it couldn't pump at all, and it failed.

He died several days later in the middle of the night. None of us had believed he would die. It put us all in a state of shock. At the funeral home, I tried to wake him up. At the church and the reception afterward, I was numb. In most ways, I stayed numb about his death for years, even though it shaped the whole rest of my life. I finished high school, I went on to the university, I grew up, I became a medical technologist and an entrepreneur, but I was nearly middle-aged before I realized how his illness and death had given me the energy, determination, and inspiration to do almost everything I've done.

There were nine kids in my family—I was in the middle—and most of us had to go to work. I didn't even try to find something at a soda fountain or a drive-in or one of the summer resorts. I went straight to the hospital to get a job in the laboratory, and I worked there all through high school. Summers, my brothers and sisters would be tanned and healthy looking, and I'd be white as a ghost. I wasn't a brain. I was a fun-loving kid with a lot of friends, sort of a hellion in many ways, but every day after school my friends would drive me to the hospital, and even though I hated to leave them, I was always serious and excited about getting back to the lab, washing test tubes, doing blood counts and urinalyses.

My first mentor was Sister Mary Grace, who ran the lab and instilled in me the basic principle of working with patients. She had taught me to draw blood as well as test it, and one day when I had finished a test she asked me for the result. "Oh, 20 or 21," I said.

"Which was it?" she asked.

"What difference does it make?" I said. "Normal is 18 to 25."

"You have to know exactly," she said. "Put down what you're doing, go out there, redraw the blood, and come back here and do it again."

So I had to go out and restick the patient and redo the test. The result I got was 20.

"It's 20!" I told her. I was furious. I didn't really enjoy sticking needles into people.

"The doctor could be basing his medication on that number," she said, "so whether it's higher or lower than last time could be critically important." Then she looked at me hard. "Whenever you do a test, I want you to pretend you're doing it on your father."

At the time, I thought it was a cruel thing for her to say; she knew how close I'd been to him. But it's something I still say to Medical Graphics employees.

"Suppose you bring a parent or a child to an emergency room," I say. "Suppose it's your daughter, and she's having trouble breathing. Suppose the nurse wheels up a piece of Medical Graphics equipment to test her with and find out why. What is it you want to feel at that moment? A sense of relief—because you helped build the best equipment in the world, because you know it gives meaningful, accurate results, because it can save your child's life."

I went to the College of St. Scholastica in Duluth because it has a good program in medical technology. On top of all the math and chemistry and anatomy, I worked my way through school in hospital labs. I never thought of it as work, I liked it. I took it for granted. My motivation was so strong that nothing discouraged me.

I *knew* where I was going. I was going to prevent heart and lung disease. I didn't talk about it. I didn't even consciously connect it with my father's death, but that was my goal. I was going to make a difference. No one should die at 47.

After college, I landed a job in the cardiopulmonary lab at the University of Minnesota Hospital in Minneapolis, and I stayed there for eight years, working, studying, and doing research. I taught myself computer programming. I couldn't afford my own computer, but my husband, Stephen, was a salesman for Tektronix, and I worked on his demo. I figured out how to turn pages of diagnostic numbers—vital capacity, total lung capacity, minute ventilation, lung diffusion, oxygen consumption, carbon dioxide production, esophageal pressure, heart rate, blood pressure, plus a dozen other parameters—into computer graphics that incorporated all of it at once. I wrote software to produce such graphics from manually entered data, and I got the best doctors I could find to help me interpret the results so I could teach others to do the same. I went to medical conventions to show doctors my software. I had no strategic sales plan. I was just excited about what I could do. Nevertheless, several doctors hired me to automate and improve their laboratories, and one day Stephen suggested I build a business on the technology I was developing.

Stephen talked to his boss at Tektronix and got him to lend me $180,000 worth of equipment to demonstrate my software at medical conventions—and then I wouldn't give it back to him. I kept it for another month and then another, on the grounds that eventually I would start selling enough Tektronix computers along with my software that it would pay off for his company as well as for me. Eventually it did.

Finally, I began working with transducers and electronic analyzers, figuring out how to translate analog data directly into digital information and computer graphics. In theory, this would allow a doctor to read and interpret dozens of pieces of intricately related information as a graphic whole—and to do it in real time, or very nearly. It would allow people with shortness of breath to go to a doctor or a hospital, breathe into an apparatus that I was going to invent, and find out immediately whether they had a heart problem or a lung problem and, in many cases, what the problem was. Much of this information could be extracted simply by knowing at what rate a person was using oxygen. But I believed I could build equipment that would measure enough parameters to determine from an analysis of the breath alone—that is to say, completely *noninvasively*—whether a person had emphysema, asthma, bronchitis, a valve problem, coronary artery disease, congestive heart failure, or one of a dozen other circulatory system diseases.

I had a mission to help save lives. I was driven to do everything I could do to realize my mission—and to do all of it myself. I was a crusader, an inventor, a salesperson, an organizer, a hustler. I had been a kind of monomaniac, unconsciously, ever since my father died. Now I was beginning to be an entrepreneur.

One day in 1979, I got a call from Dr. Stephen Boros at St. Paul Children's Hospital, who told me a baby boy had been born with a rare disorder that caused him to stop breathing whenever he fell asleep. Boros and his staff had him on a respirator, but the long-term outlook was poor. In normal people, it is the level of carbon dioxide, or CO_2, in the blood that controls the depth and frequency of breathing. Here, they had to control breathing externally, and they had to get it right. Too much CO_2 could put the baby into a coma, too little would upset his internal chemistry. Their only recourse was to check CO_2 by taking repeated blood samples, a process that was awkward, painful, slow, and invasive.

Since life on a respirator is a kind of hell in any case, some felt the baby should be allowed to die. But Boros wanted to put a pacemaker on the nerve controlling the diaphragm, which might allow him to live a reasonably normal life. To get the breathing rate just right, he needed some way of measuring the baby's oxygen and CO_2 levels noninvasively, one breath at a time, and he knew I had done similar breath-by-breath testing on cats.

"But you're talking about a baby," I objected.

"You've got to help me," he said. It was the kind of system I wanted to build eventually, and now a baby's life was at stake; Boros was just forcing the issue. I told him I might be able to put one together in as little as a month. He asked me to do it in two weeks.

I put down the phone, picked it up again, and started putting in calls to suppliers, one in the Netherlands, others in Kansas City and Seattle. I asked them to ship me—overnight express—transducers, analyzers, computers, calibrators, pumps, a pneumotachograph for measuring the rate of respiration. I put them all together Rube Goldberg-style on my dining-room table. What this collection of equipment had to do was measure oxygen and carbon dioxide accurately in each small mass of expired air, translate the results into digital information, feed these data into a computer, and render the combined results precisely, sequentially, instantly, and in a graphic form that a doctor, nurse, or technician could quickly read and understand. That may *sound* easy, but no one had ever done it before. The software alone kept me up until four in the morning ten nights in a row.

Two weeks later I called Dr. Boros and told him I was ready. He met me at the hospital. We wheeled my apparatus in on a cart, adjusted a tiny mask on Colin's face—he now had a name—and started taking measurements. Everything worked. The video screen drew graphs showing the contents of Colin's expired air, breath by breath, exactly the way it should, and we could see that his CO_2 was dangerously high. Boros cautiously turned up the pacemaker, Colin began breathing a tiny bit faster, and his CO_2 began slowly dropping into the normal range. Within two or three days, Boros and his staff were able to stabilize the baby's unconscious breathing at an adequate, sustainable level. Colin lived.

Medical Graphics was born.

An entrepreneurial business has an infancy, an adolescence, and a maturity. Entrepreneurs go through a similar kind of evolution, though the business and the person seldom develop at the same pace and in harmony from newly hatched all the way to adult. At the beginning, the entrepreneur and the business are identical. The idea, the vision, and the passion are all inside the entrepreneur, overflowing in every direction. An entrepreneur operates on the basis of abundance: grand opportunities, ambitious dreams, big plans, wide-open doors just waiting for someone to walk through them.

In my case, I saw a huge gap in the ability to diagnose heart and lung disease, and I set out to fill it. I built integrated, more compact versions of the equipment I had used on Colin. I lobbied the finest cardiologists and pulmonologists I could find and asked them to join my scientific advisory board. I wasn't shy. I'd go to medical meetings, pick out the leading doctor, insist on talking to him, tell him what

Medical Graphics was, drag him back to our booth, and make him watch while I demonstrated the equipment. As soon as he got excited—and they always did—I'd say, "You can have this very equipment in your office next week for $20,000. But what I really want is for you to tell us how to make it better, tell us what you need. I want you to work with us and help us develop it further." They couldn't say no. They never did.

I traveled constantly. I stayed alone in hotels and drove lonely back roads by myself to get to hospitals and doctors in remote locations. I'd leave my two young children at home and fly off to a meeting in California and cry all the way to the coast, thinking, "I should be home taking care of my kids." But I did it. I did everything. I developed the products, wrote software, consulted with the doctors, did marketing and sales, wrote brochures, built a company, found a board of directors, issued stock, and delegated nothing. I was a typical infant entrepreneur and then a typical adolescent.

The company moved into the go-go stage. Sales climbed over $1 million. We had profits one year and no profits the next, but our R&D efforts were continuous. We introduced new systems or new software about every six months. We built devices that could measure 144 parameters of lung and heart activity. We developed a body plethysmograph to measure total lung capacity, airways resistance, and lung elasticity, and an inexpensive spirometer to screen people quickly for lung disease at the workplace or in a doctor's office. We made equipment that helped measure and control breathing and nutrition in intensive-care units. All of these systems were noninvasive, and all were unique. For years, Medical Graphics was the only player in the field. Sales climbed over $3 million.

We broadened our focus and got into sports medicine. NASA bought our equipment to test astronauts in space. General Motors used our systems to study the effects of explosive air-bag deployment. We went after markets in Europe, the Middle East, and the Soviet Union. We continued to introduce new products. Sales climbed over $7 million. I had my finger in every pie, I was everywhere and did everything— R&D, sales, marketing, planning, finances, and outreach. I was Medical Graphics, and Medical Graphics was Kye Anderson.

Then, under pressure from my board and the stress of my own frustration, I quit as CEO.

There is an old business axiom that says that no entrepreneur can take her own company beyond $10 million in sales. According to this view, entrepreneurs are fixed in the infant or adolescent stages of personal and company development and can never progress to adulthood. As Medical Graphics began to approach that $10 million threshhold, I could see a lot of good reasons to believe the axiom was true.

In the first place, my talent was entrepreneurial, not managerial. I still burned with a kind of childish passion to save lives, to help cure heart and lung disease, to make a difference in the world.

I knew the technology, but I knew nothing about manufacturing. I knew the doctors and what they needed, but I was a marketing amateur.

Growth was too slow, and I had no idea how to plan. In fact, I never planned for anything but success. If someone said, "What do we do if we lose this order?" I'd figure he had to be mentally ill to be so negative.

I couldn't seem to get the company moving upward on an even keel. One year we'd make a profit, the next year we'd lose money. I didn't even care that much about profits. I wanted profits to keep the doors open, but I wasn't worried about bringing everything to the bottom line. What I really wanted was to get the products right for the market, so I kept putting more money into R&D. I figured if we got the products right, sales would take care of themselves.

Like so many entrepreneurs, I thought if I built a better mousetrap, the world would beat a path to my door. I didn't see the need to advertise the mousetrap and pave the path, and I certainly didn't know how. Every doctor that bought one of our systems would wonder why he'd never heard of us before. One of them had said to me, "This stuff is the best-kept secret in the medical world."

I was working myself nearly to death, but I was frustrated and losing my confidence. The company's financial health became my bugbear. Quarterly earnings and the price of our stock kept me awake nights. A couple of my board members thought we should be making 10% profits after taxes, and though our earnings fluctuated wildly, they never swung as high as 10%. The board urged me to step aside and make way for professional management. I was ready. I knew it was the right thing to do.

I was wrong.

I once heard an after-dinner speaker define entrepreneur as "a person who doesn't know any better." We all recognized ourselves and laughed. Entrepreneurs seldom do know what they're getting into when they start. They are people so fired up with a vision that they go blind to everyday realities—which is a good thing, since otherwise they would never even attempt to do the impossible things they so often succeed in doing. Moreover, entrepreneurs often lack a basic grasp of business skills. I certainly did.

But the definition is also true in another, more literal sense: entrepreneurs know nothing better than their own enterprises. They have the noblest missions and the finest products in the world. It doesn't matter if they make duct tape or artificial hearts; they believe they have what it takes to alter history. And they are right, at least for themselves and their own companies—and sometimes for history too.

In my own case, I was on a crusade to save lives by inventing and perfecting a technology that would aid the early detection and diagnosis of heart and lung disease. Maybe it's true, as some friends claim, that deep down I was still trying to save my father's life. On the surface, I was, in any case, building a company on the technology doctors needed to save the lives of patients *like* my father. The point is that it was a crusade and that I was its driving force.

I tried hard to stay away, and for more than a year I succeeded. I spent a lot of time on the phone with salespeople, working out strategies for particular customers, and I attended board meetings. I was still chairman. But despite a sense that people were losing their enthusiasm and despite the fact that we hadn't introduced a single new product or software refinement for a year, I stayed away and let the new professional managers run the show.

But then salespeople began quitting. And one day when I went to R&D to talk about our new cardiopulmonary exercise system, hardly anyone was there, and no one knew where they were. Working at home, maybe. Taking an early lunch. Out. Yet these were the people who used to chain themselves to their desks, so to speak, and work nights and weekends with enthusiasm.

I had to face the fact that the company was losing its way. We had developed a new focus on the bottom line, sales were up, a new distribution system was in place—but people didn't seem to care. And I could see why. The new distribution system focused on logistics, not on doctors and patients. The new management systems built walls between departments and emphasized hierarchy. The new improved bottom line pleased stockholders, I'm sure, but it had put out the fire in people's guts. I wanted to come back.

When I left Medical Graphics, I left behind a company with a lot of talented, motivated people, but I took away with me an intense excitement that some of my board seemed to feel the company had outgrown, or should outgrow. The board was right about one thing, the company did need to grow and mature. But maturity isn't simply a question of scrapping visions and adopting targets. People and companies that abandon all ardor and passion lose their purpose in life. Maybe I *had* been a little crazy, but I'd been crazy like a fox, crazy with determination, crazy about an idea and a vision. That kind of madness is a thing all companies desperately need and that entrepreneurs are uniquely qualified to offer.

As for the kinds of maturity I find more relevant—appreciating complexity, learning to plan, learning to learn—I'd changed in my year and a half at home. By delegating my entire business, I had discovered that I didn't need to do every single thing myself. By reading and studying a whole library of business books, I had taught myself a great deal about marketing, finance, strategy, and vision. I'd also had time to think about my own strengths and weaknesses as a manager and leader, and I had begun to come to terms with my own history as an entrepreneur and a person. In fact, I had reached some conclusions that convinced me I could run my own company not only better than I had before but better than any professional manager could hope to do.

This time I was right.

I talked to my board members one by one and persuaded the two who were least supportive to resign. I reassumed the role of CEO. I went out looking for a mentor who had built a successful company from nothing and found him in Earl Bakken, who developed the first wearable, external, battery-powered, transistorized pacemaker in 1957, founded Medtronic Inc. to produce it, and then took the company from a garage startup to $1 billion in sales in less than 35 years. By sheer persistence and good luck, I got him to join my board.

I regained my confidence. I realized that my earlier focus on R&D had been the right focus for Medical Graphics at that stage in its development. The world was not going to beat a path to our door unassisted—marketing was necessary—but without the right products for our customers' needs, a superhighway to our door wouldn't have been much help. Now that we had the products, financial success was essential for everyone: me, my board, my managers, the employees with their stock options, even our patient stockholders. Profit is a wonderful and necessary thing. But my failure to achieve 10% after-tax profits in the mid 1980s had not been a failure at all. I had been right in my willingness to postpone profits for the sake of greater investments in research and development.

I had also come to see that our insistence on the patient as our ultimate customer was the right idea. We weren't supposed to be in business to please everyone. In my opinion, we were in business to please the patient and to give doctors the tools to prevent, diagnose, and treat heart and lung disease cost effectively and noninvasively. We were patient-driven—not sales-driven, not profit-driven, not even doctor-driven—and that fact helped give us our special sense of mission and purpose.

Earl Bakken taught me that a leader's greatest obligation is to preach. Before I took my year and a half off, I had my own private sense of purpose. It drove *me*, but I communicated it to no one else. I didn't see how I could go around telling people my goal was to do away with heart and lung disease. I'd sound like a megalomaniac. My problem was that I was so passionate about the product and getting it out to doctors and hospitals that I overlooked the most important piece of the whole operation—the people in my own organization who made it all happen. When I came back to the company, I started preaching the vision to them instead of running out to sell to the doctors.

With Earl's help, I put together a statement of higher purpose, along with statements articulating a mission, eight values, and three strategies. This sounds complicated, and it is, but I didn't want to reduce everything to a single slogan or phrase. Quality, service, innovation—how do any of those words help people in a crisis? But when mission and value statements talk about filling unmet diagnostic needs, about improving the quality of patients' lives, about maintaining competitive advantage through quality and innovation, about profit, human dignity, ethics, cost-consciousness, cost-effective medicine, about listening to customers, patients, and employees—and when these values are spelled out under a banner proclaiming, as a higher purpose, "To prevent heart and lung disease, the leading causes of death and rising healthcare costs," the result is a guide to behavior, to planning, and to problem solving. I've been able to trace back every difficulty I've ever encountered at Medical Graphics, trivial as well as serious, to a violation of one of these principles.

I had been violating them myself. Our involvement in sports medicine and air bags, for example, had nothing much to do with preventing heart and lung disease and led us away from our higher purpose. I jettisoned both, along with everything else that tempted us to wander off. After all, Medical Graphics had invented everything new in cardiorespiratory diagnostic equipment since 1977—the graphic presentation of data, the breath-by-breath technique for immediate results, diffusion measurement by gas chromatography, the first fully computerized plethysmograph, the first FDA-approved expert system for the diagnosis of lung disease. Why did we want to endanger that core competence by stretching ourselves too thin?

If we were going to take our higher purpose seriously—and it had stood me in pretty good stead ever since my father died—then it seemed clear to me and the board that our future lay in prevention. We had always worked closely with doctors, feeding on their needs, ideas, and energies. They know the patients better than we do, and we know the technology. We were already doing our best to reach cardiologists, pulmonologists, asthmatologists, respiratory therapists, intensivists, and half a dozen other cardiorespiratory specialists. The next step was primary-care physicians. They see heart and lung disease before the specialists because they see the patients earlier.

The very first sign of heart and lung disease is often either shortness of breath or simple tiredness. But when people have those symptoms, they don't go to their personal cardiologist. In fact, they generally do nothing. They wait until they've got chest pains or grow so short of breath that they can't breathe normally. Then they see a physician, have some tests, and go on to a specialist, who discovers a serious problem. They wind up getting angioplasty for $10,000, or coronary bypass surgery for, say, $20,000, or a heart-lung transplant for maybe $200,000.

Our present strategic goal is to put inexpensive equipment in every general practitioner's office that can detect heart and lung disease while it can still be cured with drugs, exercise, nutrition, and other noninvasive therapies. Every time people have a physical—certainly if they're feeling short of breath or unusually tired—they'll breathe into our apparatus while performing simple exercise, and if their oxygen consumption fails to rise, then something is wrong with their circulatory systems. If such early detection prevented one single heart-lung transplant, the savings on the surgery alone would pay for thousands of doctor's-office physicals on our equipment, even at the present price of $30,000, and we're working hard to get the price down to $15,000 or $10,000 or even $5,000. With early detection, we believe we could eliminate more than 40% of surgeries and catheterizations. Our conservative estimate of this primary-care market is $1.2 billion.

When I came back as active CEO after my year and a half at home, I began for the first time telling people the story of my father's death. To my surprise, nearly everyone I worked with had a similar story—a favorite aunt who was always short of breath until she died of undiagnosed heart disease, a father who passed a physical with flying colors and collapsed and died the next day, a mother dying horribly of emphysema, a spouse or a child getting the wrong treatment in intensive care. It turned out that all of us were in it for something more than money, and for ten years I had let that sense of higher purpose go unexpressed and unfulfilled.

It may be difficult, even painful, for an entrepreneur to expose the private emotions that drive her, but it is an indispensable piece of good entrepreneurial leadership. For Medical Graphics, it is a way of bringing all our technical and business skills to bear on the medical problems closest to our hearts.

3
The Entrepreneur Sees Herself as Manager: An Interview with Lore Harp

Eliza G.C. Collins

In 1976, at the age of 32, Lore Harp had two children, a nice home, a husband, and a growing dissatisfaction with her life. Wanting "to contribute something," she asked a friend, Carole Ely, to help her market a memory board that Harp's husband, then working at Hughes Research Laboratories, had designed. What happened then is absolute American dream. Harp and Ely (and later Bob Harp) turned their $6,000 investment into a $25 million company manufacturing eight desk-top microcomputer models selling in the $4,000 to $25,000 range. Located in Thousand Oaks, California, the company went public in 1981, and according to Harp, her goal is to hit $200 million in sales by 1985.

How has Harp, chief executive officer of Vector Graphic Inc., done it? In this interview she discusses her background, her dissatisfaction with the role of housewife, the beginnings of Vector Graphic and the two women's nurturing of it, the rapid growth, and her attention to marketing, services, and support that distinguished Vector from other microcomputer companies right from the start. This success has not been without sacrifice, however. Because of her driving interest in Vector, Harp suffered the loss of friends as well as the breakup of her marriage. Being an entrepreneur is not easy at the best of times, but being female brings with it a separate set of problems. Yet if Lore Harp is an example, the difficulties might be worth it.

HBR: *Can we begin by talking a little about your background? You came to this country from Germany when you were 20. What had your life in Germany been like?*

Lore Harp: I'm the oldest and I have one younger brother. I had a very normal childhood, in what you would call "a very nice family." My father was a businessman; my grandfather, whom I respected greatly, was a very successful politician during the Weimar Republic; and my father's 75-year-old twin sister was an attorney. I respected her enormously and always admired her spontaneity, her interests in so many things, her contributions.

So you grew up with the idea that success was achievable. Did you have any sense of being different as a child?

No, but I was always tremendously strong willed. I came to the United States when I was 20 to visit friends. But then I wanted to see if I could do something on my own, so I moved to the San Francisco area. At one point, my parents felt they could starve me out and get me to come back to Germany, but I stayed.

What did you want to do?

I just wanted to see what else there was. All the people I had met and stayed with in the United States were white, Republican, and wealthy. This was 1966, and so many other things were going on that I wanted to experience. I wasn't running away, though.

I never got into a drug culture or anything of that nature; I was just terribly curious about life and what makes people tick. I had so much time ahead of me that it didn't seem a few more months out of my life would make that big a difference to what I did. I only had a visitor's visa, so I could neither go to school nor officially work. So I did all sorts of little diddly things, like babysitting.

Was it tough going?

At one point I was down to $20, but I would just not call my parents and ask them to send me any money. Somehow I always made it. I had nothing to fall back on, but I suppose I knew that if things got too tough, I could call my parents and have them send me a ticket. There was always that security factor.

The sense that you were ultimately acceptable somewhere allowed you to experiment?

Yes, yes. Even though I really didn't think in those terms, probably having that little bit of a safety valve built in deep down made me dare a few more things than I otherwise would have. Eventually I met Bob Harp, got married, and started studying anthropology—probably because of the experiences I'd had during the prior months. And then I got pregnant; I have two daughters, 12 and 10.

Were you happy being a mother at home?

I cannot stand being at home; it absolutely drives me insane. I was always doing something outside, but I never once belonged to the PTA. When we moved to the suburbs, I felt obliged to join something like Children's Hospital, but I could just not believe the time the women would spend trying to analyze the "corporate environment." It was a waste, yet they thought it was so "important." I only joined because everybody thought I was strange anyway as I would not go to the bridge club or have my fingernails done. I enjoy cooking because it's creative, but I never could stand being at home.

It didn't occur to you that you were an oddball, that something might be wrong with you?

If you don't love scrubbing plates and making little knickknacks out of dough for the kid's Christmas trees? Not at all; it never crossed my mind. So I did a stint at law school, when the children were three and five.

How did you manage that?

I didn't. I just literally could not do the reading. It was such a massive amount, and my husband was not the kind of person who would say, "Okay, I'll take over half the chores; you go ahead and study," even though he was otherwise very supportive. I tried to do everything, but I just decided I could not finish school and keep my sanity. So I took a leave of absence with the idea of continuing later. But I got so bored again. That's when we started Vector.

In studying entrepreneurs, researchers have found that one of the things that characterizes them is that they hit a plateau and feel displaced, which they relieve by taking on a new activity. This sounds true of you.

I think it was, because I had quit law school and started to play a lot of tennis. I actually became quite good at it. But just playing tennis all the time was really not quite what I had in mind either. Bob Harp had designed this memory board that was supposed to be marketed almost a year earlier through another company he was involved with, but it never came off. So he said to me, "If you're really that antsy, how would you like to market it?" I said, "Sounds fantastic."

What did he mean you were antsy?

I felt very frustrated in that I wasn't really contributing to my own expansion. I wasn't doing anything except playing tennis and cooking meals. It was not so much the monetary reward: I'd had the children, but there was something I had to do that had a different meaning.

So there was still building you wanted to do for yourself?

You know, it's funny, I was 32 at the time, and I felt, "My God, suddenly I'll be 40, the children will be gone, and where am I going to be?" That may have been the subconscious reason. See, I'm always trying something new. Now that things will be settling down here a bit, I'm going to take a class in sculpture. I want to do something unrelated to anything I've ever done.

Was it important to start Vector on your own?

Oh, yes. What it really boils down to is that I don't like to be dependent on anybody. And that has been part of the problem with my marriage—why Bob Harp and I are divorcing. I'm independent, and I think many men have a problem with that. I like going to the airport in Tokyo or someplace where you can't read anything and still get on the plane without asking a husband, "How do I get there?"

So Vector was a result of your being antsy?

That and a combination of factors. Bob Harp had designed the computer memory board, which wasn't going anywhere, so I called my friend Carole Ely and asked if she wanted to join me in this venture. Carole was very involved with her children at the time, even though she had been a bond trader before. She thought the idea was great.

With no idea of computers except what you'd picked up at home and no formal business experience, how did you begin? I've read that two days after Bob Harp suggested you market the memory board, you went down to the southern California computer show and incorporated.

That's more or less what happened. I decided to market the memory board, called the attorney to incorporate, told Bob to finish designing the board, called the chip supplier, and we were off.

Did you have trouble with suppliers?

Initially. I remember calling the western regional sales manager for one of the chip manufacturers to discuss buying a large number of memory chips. He said, "Fine. How about if we have an appointment at your office tomorrow?" I was calling from my kitchen phone. I said, "That sounds great, but we're in the process of moving right now." Really, I meant moving into the downstairs bedroom, which I was cleaning out. So I said, "Could we meet maybe over drinks at the WestLake Inn?" So we met at WestLake an hour after we had incorporated.

What happened?

He looked at Carole and me and I could just see the thought process going on in his head. "Oh, my God, what did I get myself into?" We sat down and discussed buying 50,000 chips, representing about a $75,000 purchase. We started the company with $6,000. As we sat there and talked about chips and pricing, he gave us outrageous prices. I finally said, "That's ludicrous. We need a price now, not a year from now, in order to have an impact. It has to make economic sense!" He just didn't trust us. I said to him, "If you don't sell to us, we'll find somebody else. This is a hot market. Our product is going to be in tremendous demand." But he didn't want to sell to us.

What really amuses me today, considering we started with $6,000, a lot of enthusiasm, and knowledge that we would succeed (which buys you practically nothing), is that we were able to negotiate 30-day credit terms with the vendors—with no assets.

How did you do it?

Power of persuasion. After a while, salesmen started coming to the house. As a matter of fact, I think our neighbors must have thought we had a sort of brothel going, because the salesmen would stay for half an hour and leave. They'd arrive with doughnuts in the morning, and then they'd put on a pot of coffee. And one fellow would deliver memory chips he'd picked up at the airport, and so forth, at night.

Who was doing the manufacturing?

Initially we sold kits: Carole and I sat on the floor and packed all the stuff, and UPS would come by every day to pick up and deliver the product.

Did you have difficulty getting retailers to stock Vector?

One of the reasons we were very successful initially was total instinct. Basically we treated dealers the way we would like to be treated. We wrote potential dealers whose names we had found in the various trade publications that were turning up all over the place. We started off, "Dear dealer—meet the 8K baby." That's what we called the memory board because it was attached to a mother board. We described all the merits of this particular memory board and then signed our letters—I'll never forget—"Very truly yours, Lore Harp, president; Carole Ely, vice president and secretary/treasurer," which was ridiculous because nobody signs letters secretary/treasurer. And then to be more official, I would type LH/mtf, meaning "my two fingers."

Did the letters work?

They usually resulted in dealers stocking between two and ten boards. We'd call the dealers about five days later to ask if they'd received our letter and brochure and if we could sell them a memory board. And they said, "Um, yes." Most people were so flabbergasted by the attention they got and the fact that we were women. We really capitalized on that. They all wanted to help "the girls."

How did you know that the follow-up would make the sale?

It was a question of nurturing the process along. You don't send the child off on a trip without later checking to find out if he or she got there. I'm sure there was something of a female innate protectiveness about it, wanting to take care of something we'd started. For instance, two weeks after we had sent out the memory boards COD, I would call up again and ask whether they had received the board, did they have a chance to put it together, and did they like it? And how many more did they want to order?

Were the dealers surprised?

Yes, because nobody did that. They were overwhelmed by the support. If they had a problem they would call us up, and we would sometimes call Bob at Hughes Research Laboratories, where he was working, and ask him to call a dealer. So we were troubleshooting over the phone and servicing right from the start.

So you attribute much of your success to a special concern for something down the line?

I think so. Most of our competitors were very technically oriented people who saw a tremendous opportunity and wanted the satisfaction of having little computers they could play with. But they really had no interest in following through, in marketing, in getting the word out to the world as to why the computer is great and what it can do for the customer. Not being either designers or technically oriented, we took the other road.

How did you keep up with the growth?

Well, what I would do is get bowls out of the kitchen and put all the little components in them, and my children and Carole's would put the kits together. We also hired a lot of high school kids, part-time. It was chaotic with children, dogs, cats, and neighbors' kids. By December 1976, five months after we had incorporated, we moved to a 1,200 square foot facility. We hired our first assembler and a receptionist, who was also a salesperson, order taker, and everything else. She was my next-door neighbor, Jenine Steele. And in May 1977, because things had really taken off, we moved to another facility. It was all such fun then.

It was fun, it wasn't work?

No question about it. It was really what I think I needed for my satisfaction, let's say, as a contributor of something beyond myself. For example, I remember giving my next-door neighbor her first paycheck; it was just great. Or doing some accounting. For example, we kept books and financial statements from day 1.

How did you know how to do that?

I'm not sure. That was instinct too. You have to know where your money goes. I guess it's a bit of my German nature too. Some of the companies that have gone out of business essentially kept their bills and invoices and everything else in one big box.

I don't know whether that's necessarily Germanic; it sounds more like good planning.

You need a structure to keep control of the details while you're doing something else. And even though we were operating on such a small scale, we were very organized. Things went very well, and Bob decided to design some other products. Soon we had a full-fledged computer, eventually hired some more people, and moved into a larger place. Everyone was scared. At the time, it cost us almost $17,000 a year for rent. And then we moved into this big facility, which costs $60,000 to lease. I started to look for this space in March 1980, a year and a half before we moved in. We've invested $2.3 million into this little building. I knew we were going to grow very fast.

When you were talking about your background, you said it was important to have your family to fall back on. Do you think that having a husband who had a good job allowed you to take risks?

No, because I knew I could always go out and do something. I think it was much more important for Bob Harp. He wanted to see that the company actually was off the ground before he quit Hughes. It took him a year. But we had real estate and stocks and so on, so there was other income. It was not as if we were totally dependent on the salary from Hughes. It could have helped subconsciously, though.

It sounds as if you'd have done it anyway.

Yes! We went public yesterday, I'm a million and a half dollars richer, and it's totally unimportant. Isn't that weird? You can change your clothes only so many times. Money's really not the underlying criterion. What I really enjoy is growing the company, growing people within the company, accepting the challenge of being out there, competing against other companies, and making an impact. Power may have something to do with it as well. I won't deny that.

Why did you go public?

Capital is one reason, but almost more important, I thought we needed the discipline. Some people feel they can make a lot of decisions without looking at the company's total picture, and we just cannot afford to do that anymore because of our sheer size. We have to communicate among departments, and I thought that going public was one way of signaling to people that we had to be more responsible.

Some people say that female entrepreneurs need to learn to think bigger and take more risks. Was risk taking a problem for you?

Not at all, because one of the things I can do is make very fast decisions. I plan a lot, make decisions, and am risk oriented. If I make a mistake, I acknowledge it and try not to make the mistake again. But making any decision is better than no decision at all. What makes me so mad many times during staff meetings is when people come up with reasons why something can't be done. I say, "Why don't you give me just *one* reason why it *can* be done?"

People theorize about what makes most women hold back. Many feminists say it's job and sex discrimination; other people cite psychological forces. What would you say?

Basically I'm not a feminist, even though I guess I should be because of what I'm doing. But I'm not, because I feel that most women gain acceptance from peers, male or female, by proving integrity and intelligence—not by talking about job discrimination and all sorts of other complaints. I just don't have time for that.

You mean, if you can do it, why can't everybody else?

I'm very strong in my convictions. For example, I was very firm in negotiating the stock price with the underwriters. I stood my ground and said, "You have five more minutes. We must have a deal at the end of that time or else we're going to walk." When they looked shocked, I said, "OK, that's thirty seconds."

When you started, were supportive friends important to you? You had Carole Ely of course. What about other women friends?

Well, as a matter of fact, it was bad at first. My best friend was resentful because I was very enthused and talked a lot about what we were doing at Vector. For about a year and a half we really didn't speak to each other. And then on Christmas day we both had the same thought to call, and now we're good friends again. But she was jealous, which is one of the conventional pitfalls women fall into.

So there really are sacrifices independent women make in the real world— friends, husbands?

Yes, but there are men who really want that kind of woman—not very many—but a few.

And it sounds like if you want to maintain your female friends, you have to support the belief that women should only be housewives.

Once in a while I go to a traditional occasion, say, a cocktail party, where it's the husbands who do all the work and the wives stay home. They're all intelligent women and so on, but they're not doing what I'm doing and sometimes I really have a hard time talking to them because the conversation invariably ends up on tennis, or having their fingernails done, or on something I don't relate to well anymore. I'm in a different stream.

Did being a woman make it difficult to get backing, once you'd stopped being considered just a "helpless girl"?

One question I was afraid would come up during the road show before going public was how can you, not having had prior experience or having been groomed at IBM, take the company to the next level? And I think they only posed that question because I am a woman; they would never have asked that of a man.

But isn't it reasonable for underwriters to question how you're going to take a company to the next level when you've had no experience?

We were one of the pioneers of the microcomputer explosion. The buying, as well as the selling, process in this industry is different from what it had been before for computers. Buyers were much less sophisticated; they really didn't know what they wanted. So I think principles that I may have learned at IBM, DEC, or any other computer company would probably not have served me well at all. We were dealing with a totally new element.

So how did you answer the question?

I gave a reasonable answer as to our track record and where we had gone, looked in a flirtatious way at the person, and said, "But you're not *really* holding one silly little chromosome against me." When you talk to people on a one-to-one basis, you don't run into that problem. It's only when men, especially in the investment community, are in a group that being a woman can be a problem.

Do women's business networks help?

I get invited to speak or visit a lot of different feminist-oriented groups, and as I told one of them, I'm just not interested. I said if women want to get off their duffs, they've got to get off them on their own and not suddenly start leaning on strong women when before they were leaning on strong men. To succeed you have to do it for yourself and not because somebody else is telling you to. We come into the world alone and the decisions we make, we make ourselves.

But you had role models. You had your father who was in business, your grandfather who was a politician, and your aunt. Other women might not have had somebody like that in their own backgrounds to emulate.

And that's when they become feminists. I remember being at a party three years ago where I met a woman and her husband. This woman was so aggressive; I've never seen anyone like her. She had just attended a feminist seminar, and she treated her husband so poorly, it really was appalling. She said to me, "Oh, you'd better go to this assertiveness seminar so you can do something with your life." And a friend of mine who was there said, "Well, Lore just started a company and is doing something." "Oh, then," said the aggressive one, "you should get up there and talk to other women." I said, "Listen, I have no interest in talking to a bunch of women if they come on like you. But I'm going to give you one piece of advice." I asked, "Have you gone out and gotten a job yet?" "No," she answered. "Well," I said, "if you haven't, I wouldn't treat my husband the way you do because you are still dependent on him." Two years later she is still in the same rut.

So you think the lady doth protest too much?

Many women are ranting and raving against men and taking a hard line, while I like being feminine. I like a man to push in my chair at the table. I like somebody to open the car door and bring me flowers and treat me as a woman. I think, vive la difference. I love it.

When you look at yourself in your role as CEO, what do you think you are especially good at?

I've made decisions that have been good for the company. Also I'm very people oriented. I manage by not restraining and restricting employees but by giving them the responsibility and letting them carry the ball. And people respect me for those reasons. I hold very loose reins. For example, when I'm out of town, I rarely call the office. If people are not carrying out what they're hired for, they're the wrong people to have. I was very instrumental in maintaining discipline in terms of credit and collection, but it's your treatment and attitude toward people that really tells.

How does that show itself in practice?

Well, for example, a year ago I started something called the friend-ship lunch, where every week we post a sign throughout the company and nine people can sign up to be taken to a restaurant for lunch with a different vice president or myself. My turn is every fifth week. What prompted me to do that was when I was walking through a manufac-turing floor one day; I just stood there and looked at all those people working and I thought, I really don't know any of them. I don't know what they think, what makes them tick. These people are between 18 and 30 years old, and I thought, my God, they are really much more representative of the United States than I am. And I wanted to hear what they have to say.

Did you think it was important for them to know you?

It was reciprocal, but I wanted to hear more about them, and I found if we had this lunch they'd get to know me and I'd be able to listen to what they have to say. It's vital to know how people think and function.

Do the vice presidents talk to you and tell you what was discussed at the lunch?

We get together afterward, and if there's something really critical to discuss we take it on. It's a two-way communication process: what's important to us and what's important to them. For example, every-body has stock options in the company. When we went public, I said, "I want everybody who has been hired through May 31 of 1981 to have some options in Vector." I really argued with our attorneys and underwriters about this. I said I don't care if they're assembly workers, vice presidents, directors, or other managers, I want to give options to people not according to position but according to length of stay with Vector. Some people in the assembly area have more options than a director. I tell you, we got flak for this. We're going to have a little party this afternoon to celebrate going public.

You got flak from Shearson Loeb Rhoades?

Yes, our underwriters felt that stock options are reserved for moti-vating management. I said if the assembly workers do a terrible job for Vector, the upper managers might as well be dead. I found out at a lunch that people here are extremely pleased with having options in Vector.

As you grow, how do you keep the personal touches, the service and support, that characterized Vector in the beginning?

Well, for one thing, we have a very big dealer-training effort going on, which Carole is managing.

What is the program like?

We hold several classes in our training center here, which has both a lecture hall and a "hands-on" room where salespeople from various dealerships learn how to work the computer. One class is purely technical training and lasts about four days. The other is a marketing class, to teach our master method of selling.

With that amount of training, the stores people work in would be almost like franchises.

Exactly. Selling a computer is not like selling a car or a piece of hi-fi equipment. What is really vital in this business is not battling our competitors but educating the end user. To do that, you need very knowledgeable salespeople in the distribution network. So one of our requirements is that all dealers come here for training. We also maintain four training centers across the country—in New York, San Francisco, Chicago, and Atlanta.

So what you've done is to turn into an outside function what companies such as IBM do in-house.

Yes, essentially. But look at the cost structure of our equipment. It retails from $4,000 to about $25,000 without fringes. We could not afford to have a full sales force out there selling that kind of equipment. Look at IBM's marketing of its new entry. They try to sell through the same distribution outlets we do, and that's why it's so important to support our dealers by training and advertising—and to raise their own expectations.

Do you think it's paid off?

Absolutely. Number one, we have a breadth of products to answer almost any kind of need, and two, the dealers have become so well versed about the Vector equipment that it's not necessary for them to carry other lines. They know the machines so well that they can address many different worker segments, which is a tremendous plus. We have almost 100 Vector-only dealers out of 420. These are the most successful dealers, who many times have written software to fit Vector computers.

But won't you naturally have to get more formal as you grow? For instance, do you have business plans now?

Yes, but not until last year. Making a formal business plan around our initial product, let's say a three-year or a five-year plan, would have been ludicrous. The technology, the sophistication of the outside world, and the buyers all changed very quickly, and we had to react to almost day-to-day changes. To have a formal business plan at that point would have been counterproductive, and we probably wouldn't have made it. Even now, I don't believe in more than three-year business plans—one-year detailed, three-year conceptual.

We're still in an embryonic stage in our industry, and we need to let that embryo grow; at the same time, we have a one-year detailed budget and really stick to it, because we're getting too big. But a five- or ten-year plan is an academic exercise. It's cramping, and in our kind of industry we're not about to milk the company yet. With those plans, you begin to sit back, and before you know it, you've lost your flexibility.

What about people? Can you keep the spirit alive with new employees?

We've always hired people who were more qualified than we needed at the time and who wanted to grow with us. For instance, our first vice president, Dick Tata, had run a $200 million division of Burroughs and came to Vector because he saw an opportunity as well as enthusiasm here.

Also, I want us to stay manageable. For instance, I never want to have a facility with more than 700 people in it. The business becomes too abstract past that point; you lose touch.

Hiring people with the right personality also helps.

What's a Vector personality?

Someone has to have an individual style. People who aren't faddish, who don't follow a trend. And people who want to be entrepreneurs, who can be creative on their own, people who are full of energy and ideas. But we also have a lot of company activities that get everybody together, to keep the spirit we started with. For example, to celebrate our first $2 million month, almost a year ago, we hired buses and closed the company at 11 A.M. Nobody knew where we were going. We had T-shirts made up saying "Vector Computers for the Advancement of Society." I wrote a little thank-you letter telling everybody how pleased I was and how important everybody was and handed it out with champagne as people were getting on the buses. Then we went down to the beach and played baseball.

It sounds as if you owe so much to these people that you have to show you care for them in a special way.

I feel a great sense of responsibility. When we had our company picnic and about 600 people showed up, I thought, "My God, these people all depend on the paycheck they get from Vector. What if I screw up?" I almost got depressed.

That doesn't give you pause?

No, I know I'm doing the best I can, and I'm not stupid enough to think that I can run this company forever. I try to acquire the necessary tools, and up to this point I think I'm definitely in charge, but if I feel that for the good of the company I should step down, I'll do that and let somebody else carry the ball. Maybe I'll build another company.

Do you think you could let go that easily?

It's like learning to delegate. I used to be very involved in the financial activities. First, I hired a bookkeeper, then a very good comptroller, and then a few months ago a vice president of finance. I had some problem giving that up because I'd been very involved in negotiating credit lines and in doing a lot of things in the financial department, and now he has taken over. A couple of times I interfered, but I'm over that now. I'm taking off a million different hats.

In managing the company, have you found things you're just not good at?

Oh, sure. All the time. But when I find a weakness, I usually fix it by bringing somebody in who can do what I can't. For example, that's why we hired the vice president of finance. We needed stronger financial controls, somebody who understands taxes, the new laws, implications certain requirements may have on the bottom line, and so forth. I was pretty good at the beginning, but I know when I'm out of my depth in certain areas.

So you don't have to do it all.

Oh, no. My strength is the strength of other people. Where I find weakness in others, besides myself, I bring in someone else to fill in.

Have you noticed at Vector that the men manage differently from the women?

You know, I'm basically a no-nonsense manager. I don't need a lot of frills. But there's a lot of politicking going on with the men. They are empire builders, very much in competition with each other. Yes, there is definitely a difference in style. I think there's not as much honesty among the men. When we moved into this facility, I had a "cut the crap" meeting where everybody had to talk about their projects. Just by listening to the various presentations you could tell the difference between men and women. The men all used big words and covered for each other. It was obvious. Don't get me wrong. These people are real doers, but they're maybe not quite as honest because that's how they have been bred from the word go.

It's hard to avoid stereotyping, isn't it?

Oh, yes. You know, it's really funny, talking about stereotypes. I got a letter from an employee a few weeks ago in which she congratulated me on how well Vector has done. She told me that she'd been talking to a guy about Vector, when he started on about "the awful bitch who's running the company." I sent a nice note back thanking her for the compliment and said I especially enjoyed the comment about this bitch running the company because that poor guy is either so jealous or he's so stupid that he doesn't have anything else to talk about, and I must be terribly important in his eyes.

I bet you do have a reputation for being cold.

Oh, you bet. In northern California they call me the Ice Maiden. When I heard that I said, well, if the Iron Lady is good enough for Margaret Thatcher, the Ice Maiden is good enough for me. But it really doesn't bother me because people in the company, friends, and those who are important to me know me for what I am. And that's what counts.

You and Bob Harp are getting a divorce now. Isn't that another sacrifice you've had to make?

In a sense, because what he could not cope with was my own change and growth. We always had a stormy marriage because of my very independent nature. And Bob, who's seven years older than I am, wanted to protect his little-girl wife. He didn't see that the little girl never really was a little girl. I have definitely grown up, and he has said he should have recognized that a lot earlier.

Has there been a price with your children?

Not at all. My kids are the most terrific, independent, self-sufficient little people. And I have tremendous rapport with them. The only problem is that, because of our going public, I've been traveling too much this year, about 100,000 miles. So they once said, "Mum, you're gone too much." And I said, "Sweeties, I know; I've been traveling a lot." But I'm including them where I can.

According to the literature, entrepreneurs are not supposed to make good managers, and yet you seem to be able to make that switch. I'm wondering whether it's because your original allegiance was not to the product but to the company?

I never thought about it in those terms, but that's probably a very astute assessment. I was able to take a closer look at the company structure and organizational development. Right now the product is obviously very important to me, but the initial challenge, which was more important, was marketing and getting the product recognized. There has been a tremendous amount of stress lately around the company to keep both in tune because of the move to this building.

Why was the move so stressful?

People felt out of place, two of the founders were getting a divorce, and we were going public. I didn't want to lose any of the momentum within the company in terms of sales. It was important to maintain our growth pattern.

What do you want to do for yourself?

I want to take the company to be about a $200 million company by 1985. You want to have that $200 million party. You better believe it!.

Do you enjoy it as much as when you started?

Even more, because I've gotten out of some of the operational things. I remember, for example, going out to shipping to pack boxes, writing checks, talking to vendors—all at the same time. Today I really enjoy the planning activities, the streamlining, bringing people in who can carry that next responsibility.

So you enjoy the shaping?

Yes. I think that's why I want to take up sculpting. You mold and sculpt from your own conceptual sense of how things ought to be. That's really what I enjoy. As the company grows, I like the challenges, which are getting much bigger. Where once I made a decision for a $10,000 item, now I'm looking at hundreds of thousands, or millions, of dollars. And if you make a mistake you can really be in a lot of deep water. But I enjoy the molding, the strategy, the planning.

When you started, did you think you'd succeed to this degree?

Never gave it any thought that it couldn't be done. Maybe I *should* have a chromosome test.

About the Contributors

Kye Anderson is chairman, CEO, and president of Medical Graphics Corporation, a company she founded 16 years ago in St. Paul, Minnesota.

Eliza G.C. Collins was senior editor, planning, of the *Harvard Business Review* when her article was published. She then became a senior editor of the Harvard Business School Press. She now is head of HBWT Associates of Cambridge, Massachusetts, a consulting firm specializing in issues concerning women at work. She is the author of *Dearest Amanda . . . An Executive's Advice to her Daughter*, coauthor of *The Portable MBA*, and editor of *The Executive Dilemma: Handling People Problems at Work*.

Rosemarie Greco is president, CEO, and director of CoreStates First Pennsylvania Bank.

Rosabeth Moss Kanter holds the Class of 1960 Chair as Professor of Business Administration at the Harvard Business School. She served also as editor of the *Harvard Business Review* from 1989 through 1992. Her books include *The Challenge of Organizational Change*, 1992; *When Giants Learn to Dance*, 1989; and *The Change Masters*, 1983.

Gary Loveman is assistant professor at the Harvard Business School, where he specializes in entrepreneurial management. His research has focused on privatization in Poland.

Nancy A. Nichols is senior editor at the *Harvard Business Review*. A former reporter for the *MacNeil/Lehrer Newshour*, she has written articles for *HBR, Working Woman, The Christian Science Monitor, The Chicago Tribune,* and *Inc.*

Daniel Niven is case production manager at the Harvard Business School Publishing Corporation.

Kathleen Reardon is associate professor of management and organization at the University of Southern California and author of *Persuasion in Practice.* She also advises on negotiation, persuasion, and organizational change.

Judith B. Rosener is a professor in the Graduate School of Management at the University of California, Irvine and coauthor with Marilyn Loden of *Workforce America: Managing Employee Diversity As a Vital Resource,* 1990.

At the time his article was published in the *Harvard Business Review,* **Robert Schrank** was a product specialist for the Ford Foundation, where his major responsibility was to monitor and evaluate training and related educational programs.

Felice N. Schwartz is founder and former president of Catalyst, a national not-for-profit research and advisory organization that works with business to affect change for women. She is the author of *Breaking with Tradition—Women and Work, The New Facts of Life.*

Sally Seymour is a communications specialist at The Boston Consulting Group.

Nan Stone is the Program Executive of the Harvard Business School Publishing Corporation's Management Production Group. Before that she was managing editor of the *Harvard Business Review.*

HBR **Editors Past and Present**: The 12 articles in this book were the result of many years of work by many *HBR* authors and editors. Several stand out: Rosabeth Moss Kanter, who was the first female editor of *HBR* is a pioneer in the field, an inspiration, and a terrific role model. While at *HBR* she practiced what the magazine preached, creating an environment where talented editors could combine successful work and happy home lives.

Geraldine E. Willigan edited "The Ways Women Lead" and also played a role in preparing Kathleen Reardon's "The Memo Every Woman Keeps in Her Desk" for publication. Nan Stone, whose essay "Mother's Work" is included in this volume, is one of those rare women who worked part-time and returned to a series of hard-won and well-deserved promotions until she virtually ran *HBR* as managing editor.

Senior Editor Thomas Teal lovingly oversaw Felice Schwartz's "Management Women and the New Facts of Life," and Kye Anderson's "The Purpose at the Heart of Management." Alan Webber, a former editorial director of the magazine, alternately vexed and coached the women on his staff into producing thought-provoking pieces on the topic of women and work.

INDEX

Affirmative action
  compliance with company program, 61
  elements of plan for, 51–52
  involvement of employees in, 54
  training and, 56–57
Assumptions, about progress of women, 104
Attitudes
  of couples toward home responsibilities, 107–108
  discriminatory practices and, 59

Bakken, Earl, 152, 153
Best Companies for Women, The (Zeitz & Dusky), 138
Boyd, Bill, 26
"Bridge club," 15
Business plan, and entrepreneurship, 171
Butterfield, D. Anthony, 5–6

Caplan, Frieda, 15, 19
Career-and-family women, 94–95
Career development
  career-family continuum and, 91, 92–95
  child rearing and, 89
  discriminatory practices and, 51
  hour-based measures of commitment and, 109, 110–111, 123–124, 126
Career-family continuum, 91. *See also* Career-and-family women; Career-primary women
Career opportunities
  crises and, 11–12, 22
  leadership style and, 20–21

Career-primary women, 92–94
Carli, Linda L., 10
Child care, 96, 98–99
Children
  as management education, 110
  parental time with, 105–107, 124–125
  women's desire for, 104–105
Clients
  part-time legal partnership and, 120, 124
  prejudices of, 61
Cloherty, Patricia M., 16
Comeau, Donald J., 51–52
Commitment, hour-based measures of, 109, 110–111, 123–124, 126
Communication, 168–169
Compensation, 104, 127
Confidentiality. *See* Privacy, and sexual harassment cases
Connor, Joseph, 9
Corporate culture
  career-family continuum and, 91
  change in, 137–140
  discriminatory, 137
  employee commitment to, 139–140
  entrepreneurs and, 151
  feedback loops in, 82–83
  traditional values in, 52–55, 135
Corporate goals
  career-and-family women and, 94–95
  importance of women's success and, 92
  loss of women employees and, 83–84
  sexual harassment and, 67, 69
Corporate mission, 153–155
Corporate policy
  vs. company atmosphere, 76–77

Corporate policy *(continued)*
  costs of women in management and,
    88
  on part-time partners, 117, 118, 119,
    121, 125–127
  promotion discrimination and, 49, 59
  sexual harassment and, 65–66, 67–69,
    72–73
  support for, 49, 55, 60
Costs
  child care and, 98
  turnover and, 87, 118, 124
  of women in management, 87–88,
    100–101
Coulson, Zoe, 52–55
Counseling, and sexual harassment, 68
Credibility, 10, 20
Credit, giving, 18–19
Crisis, and opportunities for women,
  11–12, 22

Devaluing experiences, 77
Digital, 72
Discrimination
  affirmative action plan and, 51–52
  discussion of, vs. action, 165–166,
    167–168
  women's economic status and, 104
Domestic responsibilities
  attitudes of couples toward, 107–108
  career commitment and, 109
  individual ways of handling, 108–109
  options for dealing with, 110–111
  paternal involvement with, 109
  public policies and, 109–110
  as woman's role, 159
Dresser, Laura J., 4
Dusky, Lorraine, 138

Economic status of women, 104
Egalitarian couples, 108
Elliott, Susan S., 16, 17, 18
Ely, Carole, 157, 161, 166, 170
Ely, Robin J., 11
E-mail, 69, 71–72
Enthusiasm
  entrepreneurship and, 151–152
  interactive leadership and, 19–20
Entrepreneurship
  business evolution and, 148–150
  corporate leadership on gender issues
    and, 80–81
  managerial role and, 150, 157–175
  maturity of organization and, 151–152
  in medical technology, 143–155

Equal opportunity
  management and, 56–58, 61
  promotion process and, 60
Exclusionary practices, 82–83
Expectations
  gender differences related to, 88, 89–90
  glass ceiling metaphor and, 90
  of women, 89–90, 105

Family-career conflict. *See also*
  Career-and-family women;
  Career-family continuum; Child
  care; Maternity
  flexible scheduling and, 116
  men vs. women leaders and, 14
  part-time work policies and, 121–122,
    123–125
  women's domestic responsibilities and,
    107–111
  women's economic inequality and,
    104–107
Feedback loops, 82–83
Femininity, and managerial success, 9–10
Feminism, 167–168
Fidelity Bank, 133, 136, 138, 140, 141
Flexible scheduling
  career-and-family women and, 94, 95,
    96–98
  promotion and, 113–128
Freedom
  career-family choice and, 101
  women's employment expectations
    and, 89–90
Friendship lunch, 169
Fuchs, Victor, 103–107

Garron, Lee Chester, 72–73
Gender differences, categories of, 88. *See
  also* Sexual stereotypes; Traditional
  values
Generic approaches
  sexual harassment and, 68
  working environment issues and, 79
Glass ceiling metaphor, 90
Glovsky, Richard D., 79–80
Godfrey, Joline, 80–81
Goldstein, Marilyn, 123–124
Grace, Sister Mary, 145
Greco, Rosemarie B., 131–141

Hahn, Kurt, 26–27
Hall, D. Timothy, 125–127
Harp, Bob, 160, 161, 164, 174
Harp, Lore, 157–175

Harragan, Betty Lehan, 6
Helgesen, Sally, 7–8
Hiring, and entrepreneurship, 171–172
Hochschild, Arlie, 103, 107–111
Hopkins, Ann, 9
Human resources
  development plan for, 126–127
  management responsibility and, 61–62
  promotion process and, 57–58
  sex discrimination complaint and,
    41–51, 52, 55–56
  sexual harassment cases and, 68
Humor, sexist, 77

Immaculata College, 132–133
Inclusion, 15–17
Income, of men vs. women leaders, 14.
  See also Compensation
Information sharing, 15, 17–18, 21
Interactive leadership
  as advantageous for organizations,
    21–23
  behavior patterns in, 14, 15–20
  as feminine, 23
  roots of women's use of, 20–21
International Women's Forum (IWF),
  13–14, 21
Investment banking, interactive
  leadership in, 19, 20
IWF. *See* International Women's Forum
  (IWF)

Jackman, Jay M., 81–83
Japan, sexual harassment in, 69–70
Job-grading systems, 137
Job posting, 56
Job segregation. *See also* Sexual
  stereotypes
  Rosie the Riveter and, 4–5
  women's economic status and, 104
Job sharing, 97, 122

Kanter, Rosabeth Moss, 5, 9, 11
Kossoudji, Sherrie A., 4

Landauer, Sally C., 118–120
Law. *See* Legal compliance
Leadership. *See also* Managerial role; Top
  management
  combination of styles in, 17
  command-and-control, 5–6, 9–10, 14,
    22, 23
  diversity of styles and, 13, 21–23

entrepreneurial, 143, 153–155
gender differences in style and, 13–14
interactive, 14, 15–20
Lee, R. Marilyn, 55–58
Legal compliance
  affirmative action and, 57
  sexual discrimination action threats
    and, 61
  sexual harassment suits and, 71
Loveman, Gary W., 113–128

Machismo, 36
Machung, Anne, 103, 107–111
Managerial role. *See also* Leadership; Top
  management
  as defined by masculine traits, 5–6,
    9–10, 93
  double bind for women in, 9–10
  entrepreneurship and, 150, 157–175
  teaching as, 131–133, 138
  women acting like men in, 6–7, 9
Marineau, Philip A., 80
Masculinity, and managerial role, 5–6
Maternal metaphor, 7–9
Maternity
  gender differences related to, 88
  male corporate culture and, 6–7
  management of, 95–96
  women in top management and, 90
Maternity leave
  companies' experiences with, 99–100
  management of, 95–96
Mayden, Barbara Mendel, 123–125
Medical Graphics, 143–155
Medtronic Inc., 152
Meetings, 77
Men
  family-career conflict and, 116, 118,
    124–125
  parental leave for, 98, 99
Merck, 122
Meritocracy, 135
Middle management, career-and-family
  women in, 94–95
"Mommy Track," 6–7, 124. *See also*
  Career-and-family women

Networking
  feminist consciousness-raising and,
    167–168
  issues facing women and, 79–80,
    81–82
Nichols, Nancy, 3–12
Niven, Daniel, 63–73
Nurturing skills, 7–9

Offensive behaviors. *See* Sexual
   harassment
Old boy network
   company atmosphere and, 77
   financial backing and, 167
   promotion discrimination and, 43, 44,
      47, 49, 58–59
Organizational change, and
   opportunities for women, 22–23
Outward Bound rafting expedition, 25–37

Pachis, Sister Maria, 132–133
Parental leave for men, 98, 99
Participation, 15–17
Partnership, part-time, 113–128
Part-time employment
   career-and-family women and, 97
   corporate partnership and, 113–128
   second-shift issues and, 108–109
Performance evaluation, 138
Personal life, and promotion decisions,
      44–45, 47–48, 50, 53–54
Pfizer, 89
Plateauing
   cost of, 87
   women in top management and, 90
Posner, Joseph, 58–60
Powell, Gary N., 5–6
Power
   male perceptions of women managers
      and, 35–37
   sharing of, in interactive leadership
      style, 17–18, 21
Pratt, Edmund, 89
Price Waterhouse, 9
Privacy, and sexual harassment cases,
      69, 71–72
Promotion process
   discriminatory practices and (case
      study), 41–62
   evaluation criteria and, 125–126
   human resources department and,
      57–58
   job posting and, 56
   part-time status and, 113–128
Public policy, and working families,
      109–110

Quaker Oats, 80
Qualifications
   promotion discrimination and, 46,
      49–50, 55
   relevant, 60–61

Reardon, Kathleen, 75–84
Recognition, 18–19
Recruitment
   family policies and, 120, 125, 126
   proportion of women in pool, 91–92
Relationships, between men and women
      managers, 35–37
Research and development, and
      company evolution, 152
Responsibility
   delegation of, 172–173
   of entrepreneurs to employees, 172
   of managers in sexual harassment
      situations, 72–73
   promotion decisions and, 61–62
Retaliation, and sexual harassment, 69,
      73
Reverse discrimination, 47, 57, 58
Rhode, Deborah L., 9–10
Risk
   female entrepreneurs and, 165
   interactive leadership style and, 17, 18
   openness about women's issues and,
      75–84
Rogers, T. Gary, 60–62
Roles, and gender differences, 88, 89. *See
      also* Managerial role
Rosener, Judy B., 13–23
Rothman, Claire, 16, 19
Rowe, Mary P., 67–69
Rynd, Mary Jane, 17, 19

Schrank, Robert, 25–37
Schwartz, Felice N., 6–7, 87–101, 110
Second Shift, The (Hochschild and
      Machung), 103, 107–111
Seku hara, 70
Self-worth, 18–19
Sex discrimination suit
   at Fidelity, 136–137
   handing of threats of, 55–56, 59–60
Sexual harassment
   case of, 63–65
   as company issue, 67, 69
   formal action and, 68
   informal interventions and, 68
   long-term solutions for, 66–67
   management of, 50, 65–73
   mandatory policies and, 67, 71
   options and, 65–66, 68
   short-term solutions for, 66
   unintentional, 72
   victim's responses to, 68, 70
Sexual stereotypes, 8–9, 11–12
   entrepreneurs and, 173–174

promotion discrimination and, 43–44, 48, 55, 56–57
  training and, 56–57
  work environment and, 93–94
Seymour, Sally, 41–62
Shearson Loeb Rhoades, 170
Simms, Marsha E., 120–121
Single mothers, 104–105, 106
Socialization
  gender differences and, 88
  leadership style and, 20–21
Sports metaphor, 6
Steele, Jenine, 163
Steinem, Gloria, 83–84
Stock options, 169–170
Stone, Nan, 103–111
Support
  career-and-family women and, 96–99
  female entrepreneurs and, 166
  women managers and, 35–37

Taga, Mikiko, 69–70
Tata, Dick, 171
Teaching, as managerial role, 131–133, 138
Tectronix, 146
Top management. *See also* Leadership; Managerial role
  communication of corporate values and, 54–55, 59
  corporate change and, 80, 81
  critical mass of women in, 11–12
  leadership in women's issues and, 99
  microcomputer entrepreneur and, 157–175
  part-time status and, 113–128
  suitability of women to, 90
  woman banking CEO and, 131–141
  woman medical technology entrepreneur and, 143–155
  women in, and sexist working environment, 75–84
Traditional values. *See also* Sexual stereotypes
  corporate culture and, 52–55
  suggestions for dealing with, 54–55
  women's domestic responsibilities and, 108
  women's expectations and, 90, 105
  women's relationships to other women and, 166
Training programs
  for computer dealers, 170–171

development of, by Rosemarie Greco, 134–135, 134–136
sexual harassment and, 68, 72
for supervisors, and equal opportunity, 56–57
"Transactional" leadership, 14
"Transformational" leadership, 14
Transitional couples, 108
Trosin, Walter R., 121–122
Turnover, 87, 118, 124

Undermining of women. *See also* Work environment
  difficulty of environment change and, 81–83
  by men in power, 35–37
  in women's own communications, 10

Vector Graphic Inc., 157, 159, 160–165, 166, 169–170
Vladeck, Judith P., 70–72

Wage gap, 104
Wang, Cheryl, 65–67
Weil, John P., 118
Women business owners. *See* Entrepreneurship
Women managers
  career-family continuum and, 92–95
  male undermining of, 35–37
Women's Quest for Economic Equality (Fuchs), 103–107
Workaholic culture, 123–124
Work environment
  career-primary women and, 93–94
  discriminatory atmosphere in, 55, 56–57
  equal oportunity for advancement and, 55–58
  harassment and, 67
  memo on issues facing women in, 75–84
  number of women business owners and, 80–81
  sexist atmosphere in, 75–84, 93–94
Work-family conflict. *See* Family-career conflict
Work force, proportion of women in, 55

Zeitz, Baila, 138

2AKF 2334 5/8/94 NW

HD6054.4
U6R43
1994